WHEN's
NEW TEACHER

28 STRATEGIES
to Align Your Good Intentions
with Your Teaching Practices

Elizabeth Soslau, Ph.D.

free spirit
PUBLISHING

Copyright © 2025 by Elizabeth Soslau

All rights reserved under International and Pan-American Copyright Conventions. Unless otherwise noted, no part of this book may be reproduced, stored in a retrieval system, or transmitted in any form or by any means, electronic, mechanical, photocopying, recording, or otherwise, without express written permission of the publisher, except for brief quotations or critical reviews. For more information, go to freespirit.com/permissions.

Free Spirit, Free Spirit Publishing, and associated logos are trademarks and/or registered trademarks of Teacher Created Materials. A complete listing of our logos and trademarks is available at freespirit.com.

Library of Congress Cataloging-in-Publication Data
Names: Soslau, Elizabeth, author.
Title: When you're the new teacher : 28 strategies to align your good intentions with your teaching practices / Elizabeth Soslau, Ph.D.
Other titles: When you are the new teacher
Description: Huntington Beach : Free Spirit Publishing, an imprint of Teacher Created Materials, Inc, [2024] | Includes bibliographical references and index.
Identifiers: LCCN 2024009317 (print) | LCCN 2024009318 (ebook) | ISBN 9798885545099 (paperback) | ISBN 9798885545105 (ebook) | ISBN 9798885545112 (epub)
Subjects: LCSH: Student teachers--Training of--United States--Handbooks, manuals, etc. | First year teachers--Training of--United States--Handbooks, manuals, etc.
Classification: LCC LB2157.U5 S6574 2024 (print) | LCC LB2157.U5 (ebook) | DDC 371.1020973--dc23/eng/20240620
LC record available at https://lccn.loc.gov/2024009317
LC ebook record available at https://lccn.loc.gov/2024009318

Free Spirit Publishing does not have control over or assume responsibility for author or third-party websites and their content. At the time of this book's publication, all facts and figures cited within are the most current available. All telephone numbers, addresses, and website URLs are accurate and active; all publications, organizations, websites, and other resources exist as described in this book; and all have been verified as of March 2024. If you find an error or believe that a resource listed here is not as described, please contact Free Spirit Publishing.

Permission is granted to reproduce the pages included in the List of Reproducible Pages (page ix) or in the digital content that goes with this book for individual, classroom, and small group use only. Other photocopying or reproduction of these materials is strictly forbidden. For licensing and permissions information, contact the publisher.

Edited by Marjorie Lisovskis
Cover and interior design by Mayfly Book Design

Printed by: 70548
Printed in: China
PO#: 12899

Free Spirit Publishing
An imprint of Teacher Created Materials
9850 51st Avenue North, Suite 100
Minneapolis, MN 55442
(612) 338-2068
help4kids@freespirit.com
freespirit.com

For Harry and Chris, my true loves and biggest cheerleaders

Contents

List of Figures viii

List of Reproducible Pages ix

Introduction 1

Why This Book? 2

Who Is the Book For? 2

Scope and Organization 3

How to Use the Book 4

Author's Perspective: Ideas That Underlie the Book's Strategies 5

Two Common Truths 8

Chapter One: Getting Your House in Order   9

Strategies for School Year Preparation

Strategy 1: Unearth Students' Funds of Knowledge 10

Strategy 2: Discover Community Assets 12

Strategy 3: Identify Family Expectations 15

Strategy 4: Help Students Learn Family Expectations and Set Goals 21

Chapter Two: Collaboration Is Essential   39

Strategies for Building Relationships with Families, Colleagues, and Administrators

Strategy 5: Invite Family Adults to Share Their Expertise with the Class 40

Strategy 6: Guide Students to Reflect on the Family Visits 43

Strategy 7: Use a Four-Step Framework to Navigate Teacher-Family Communications . . . 45

Strategy 8: Use Peer Observations to Build Partnerships with Colleagues 48

Strategy 9: Form or Join a Teacher Inquiry Group 52

Strategy 10: Develop Relationships with Administrators 58

Chapter Three: Love and Care in Teaching ⋅ 69

Strategies for Affirming Student Identity and Belonging

Strategy 11: Recognize the Importance of Demonstrating Love and Care for Students . . 70

Strategy 12: Anchor Your Classroom with Mirrors, Windows, and Sliding Glass Doors . . . 71

Strategy 13: Help Students Express and Share Their Identities 73

Strategy 14: Help Students Consider How They See Themselves and How Others
See Them 76

Strategy 15: Make All Classroom Spaces Affirming Places 79

Strategy 16: Connect with Journaling and Letter Writing 81

Strategy 17: Set Norms Together to Build a Classroom Community 84

Strategy 18: Have a Shout-Out Box for Student Affirmations 86

Chapter Four: Embracing Opportunities for Growth ⋅ 95

Strategies for Navigating Challenges, Building Expertise, and Sustaining Joy

Strategy 19: Follow a Recipe for Addressing Problematic Situations with Colleagues 96

Strategy 20: Make Help-Seeking a Key Part of Your Professional Practice 101

Strategy 21: Embolden Yourself to Contribute Expertise 103

Strategy 22: Learn Ways to Manage Stress, Ward Off Burnout, and Find Joy
in Teaching 105

Chapter Five: Moving Out and Beyond ⋅ 115

Strategies for Transitioning to a New Classroom, School, or Role

Strategy 23: Reflect and Plan to Make Goodbyes Meaningful 116

Strategy 24: Expand Your Portfolio 118

Strategy 25: Prepare for New Beginnings 121

Strategy 26: Set Yearlong Aspirations for Curriculum and Learning 122

Strategy 27: Visit and Start Planning for Your New Space 124

Strategy 28: Make Time for Summer Learning 125

A Final Word of Encouragement **131**

Acknowledgments **133**

Appendix: Expert Perspectives: Foundations for Teaching and Learning **135**

References **137**

Index **139**

Digital Resources **145**

About the Author **147**

List of Figures

1.1: Fifth Grade Funds of Knowledge Reflection Chart 11

1.2: Concentric Map of Community Assets 13

1.3: Community Asset Planning 14

1.4: Student Feelings Tally 17

1.5: Parent-Reported Student Challenges/Areas of Acceleration and
Expected Supports 18

1.6: Family Communication Preferences Chart 19

1.7: Family Follow-Up Letter 20

2.1: Family Expertise Planning Chart 41

2.2: Family Participation Invitation 42

2.3: Inquiry Group Invitation 53

2.4: Summary of a Basic Protocol for a Teacher Inquiry Group 54

2.5: Framing a Problem of Practice 55

3.1: This Is Me 75

3.2: Student Identity Data Chart 80

3.3: Classroom Spaces Inventory 80

3.4: Prompts for Two-Way Journaling 82

3.5: Sample Norms Word Cloud 85

3.6: Sample Seventh Grade Classroom Norms 86

4.1: Points of Collaboration Reflection Questions 106

5.1: Sample Administrator Report Details 119

5.2: Sample Portfolio Tracking Form 120

List of Reproducible Pages

All About Me: Special Skills and Interests 26

Funds of Knowledge Reflection Chart 27

Concentric Map of Community Assets 28

Community Asset Planning 29

Family Expectations Questionnaire 30

Parent-Reported Student Challenges/Areas of Acceleration and Expected Supports 32

Family Communication Preferences Chart 33

My Questions for a Treasured Adult 34

My Goal for School 36

Planning and Reaching My Goal 37

Family Expertise Planning Chart 64

Peer Observation Form 65

Reflection on a Problem of Practice: Questions to Consider 66

What's the Dilemma? Summary and Details about a Problem of Practice 67

This Is Me 88

Who Is the Me That Others See? 89

Student Identity Data 91

Classroom Spaces Inventory 92

Norms Questionnaire 93

Redressing Missed Opportunities 111

Points of Collaboration Reflection Questions 112

My Plan for Joyful Task Completion 113

Peer Report 127

Administrator Report 129

Portfolio Tracking Form 130

Introduction

TEACHER SPOTLIGHT

Starting Out

"When I first started teaching, I was fearful of being majorly unprepared. I was fresh out of my undergraduate program and felt so certain I was nowhere near prepared to start teaching. My biggest fear was being inadequate to teach such young, inquisitive minds. I came to learn that confidence is a big part of teaching. I felt more confident when I asked our instructional team for help, having them come into my room, watch a lesson, and then give me pointers on things to change or tweak. Overall, while my fear was valid, I was able to overcome it and learn more about myself in the process."

• • •

"I couldn't wait to set up my room and get started teaching. Soon after being hired, I found out that I would be teaching first grade. I was terrified because I had no idea what to do with little ones. I got started right away, planning out my classroom and looking up different websites for ideas on how to teach first grade and what to expect. On the first day of school, they all came in with a smile and an excitement for learning. We spent most of the day getting to know each other, exploring the classroom and materials while creating an environment where they felt safe and loved. We all made it through our first day—they didn't want to go home, and I didn't want them to leave either. It was at that moment that I knew I could teach first grade and love it."

• • •

"I was so excited for my first teaching job! I always dreamed of being a teacher, and to finally have my own classroom was a dream come true! It was also a bit surreal that I was now in charge of teaching these 120 students. I was eager to show them how cool math can be and to have them see that they could all be successful in math!"

We each begin our teaching journey with a clear set of aims. We want to teach well so our students thrive. We commit to becoming lifelong learners. We are armed with good intentions. Too often, though, many of us are confronted with the hard realities of schooling: mandated curricula, scripted lesson plans, inauthentic instructional materials, systems that hinder parental collaboration, schedules that hamper our attempts to reflect and improve our teaching . . . the list goes on. What practices can we enact that help us navigate these realities? How do we make good on our good intentions?

As a longtime teacher educator and former public-school teacher, I have a keen sense of what it feels like to want to teach well, yet not feel fully equipped to do so. Over the years, I often craved a resource for self-directed, self-paced professional learning that I could use to improve my practice.

Importantly, as a classroom teacher, I wanted to implement teaching practices that helped me fulfill my intentions to meet my students where they were, to show that I valued their identities and skills, to make their learning meaningful and authentic, and to make what we did in the classroom matter. As a teacher educator, I wanted a practical and empowering resource my teacher candidates could carry with them as they began their careers and as they moved forward, with ideas they could easily digest and implement in their classrooms from the start. I could never find quite the right guidebook, so I decided to write it.

Why This Book?

There are numerous books offering strategies for lesson planning, coordinating lessons to meet curriculum requirements, and organizing the classroom to meet these requirements. The strategies in *When You're the New Teacher* focus on tasks and activities that cut across—and move beyond—planning, instruction, and classroom management. Great teaching requires strong relationships among teachers, colleagues, students, families, and communities. Teachers who engage in relationship building know how to navigate challenges and overcome barriers. They leverage their students' skills and interests as legitimate curricular starting points and create context for deep learning, reflection, and student-centered instruction. This book addresses those critical teaching qualities, offering practical, step-by-step activities to help you know and understand students and families, build effective relationships with coworkers and supervisors, and put love and care at the heart of your teaching.

Who Is the Book For?

New teachers want to become excellent teachers. Excellent teachers are always trying to get better at teaching. This book is meant to help you as a teacher starting out, or wherever you are along your teaching path. It invites you to reflect on the course you want to set for yourself and to grow professionally from the start and as your career progresses.

- As a teacher candidate or a beginning teacher, you can use the book to prepare for your first year of teaching; to implement activities to get to know students, their families, and the surrounding community; to practice student-centered instructional approaches; and to reflect on your teaching toward the goal of continuous improvement.

- If you are a more experienced teacher moving to a new school, the book can help you get to know your new colleagues and deepen your skill set by thinking through ways to incorporate culturally responsive practices in your daily repertoire and engage more productively with colleagues around complex teaching topics.

- Teacher educators, induction leaders, teacher mentors, student teaching field supervisors, and instructional coaches: this book is for you as well. Use it as a professional learning tool to guide teacher-learners through activities and reflective exercises to improve their practice.

Scope and Organization

Five chapters present twenty-eight strategies to help you prepare, plan, act, and reflect on what you're learning, what's working, what you want to change, and how to go about it.

Chapter 1. Through four interrelated strategies, this chapter walks you through how to learn about students' lived experiences and integrate them into curriculum planning, become familiar with and determine how to make use of community assets, collect information about students' families, and help your students set and attain goals.

Chapter 2. Here you'll find ways to partner with school stakeholders and build relationships to enhance your students' learning experiences and your own. The chapter's six strategies offer activities that will help you plan for building positive relationships with families, colleagues, and administrators; craft ways to engage parents as experts in your classroom; partner with teaching peers to improve your instructional practices; and maintain a strong working relationship with your principal.

Chapter 3. Understanding the role of love and care in the classroom is addressed in chapter 3. Eight strategies include easy-to-follow directions for classroom-based activities to assist you in creating identity-affirming lessons and spaces, strengthening your classroom community, and expressing your respect and care for your students.

Chapter 4. This chapter presents four strategies to navigate challenges while identifying opportunities to develop your collaborative expertise. You will learn how to address

Introduction

problematic decisions, remarks, or actions of other professionals and colleagues; seek help when you need it; build and contribute your own expertise; grow your tolerance for vulnerability; bring joy to required tasks; and support your emotional well-being.

Chapter 5. Teaching involves a host of transitions. Chapter 5 offers six strategies to use as you move from one teaching situation to another. In addition to learning how to plan to enter or reenter the job market or prepare to move to a different school, you will complete an exit strategy action plan that includes how to thank school stakeholders, how to lovingly say goodbye to students, and ways to request documentation of your own accomplishments.

Throughout the chapters, you will find real-life examples, sample dialogues, and stories from educators and students. At the end of each chapter are forms you can print or download to guide your planning and reflection.

How to Use the Book

When You're the New Teacher is self-paced and meant to be used regularly and year after year. My hope is that you will treasure this book as a personal reflective toolbox that enables you to systematically improve your teaching practice throughout your tenure as a practitioner. Alongside the book, be sure to keep a dedicated notebook or digital file for the journaling and reflective writing that are key to many of the book's activities.

Learning about teaching can be overwhelming, so I encourage you to pace yourself in a way that suits you best. It's fine to focus on the strategies one or two at a time. Use the table of contents as a menu, selecting chapters and strategies that fit your needs at any given time. For example, at the start of a new school year, begin with chapter 1 and find tools to learn about and consider how to incorporate what your students already know into your lessons, unearth families' academic desires, and locate neighborhood resources to connect your classroom with the community. If it is the middle of the school year and the culture and climate of your classroom could use a refresh, you might jump to chapter 3 for activities to build community. If you just found out that you will be moving to a new school, open to chapter 5 to get tips for making a smooth transition. Or perhaps you find yourself in a difficult debate with a colleague about how to approach a controversial classroom topic; chapter 4 gives you conversation protocols to navigate this challenge.

You can also use the book as part of professional learning community with a small group of teachers who wish to explore their instructional decision-making and work collectively to implement ideas from the book to improve their practice. In addition to the classroom activities and teacher reflections in the first three chapters, chapter 4 will be helpful in improving collaboration within and across groups of teachers such as grade groups and small learning communities.

If you are a teacher educator working with novice teachers or a teaching coach who supports teachers across the career lifespan, you will find many helpful insights to share with your mentees throughout this book. During student teaching or methods courses, you can assign activities based on an instructional area of need identified during field observations.

The book can also serve as curriculum material for student teaching seminars, clinical practice sites, or induction programs. Instructors in teaching seminars can assign chapters and activities for teachers to try out in their own classrooms; the teachers can then report back, sharing their experiences and insights on how they adapted any of the tools to fit the needs of their educational context.

Author's Perspective: Ideas That Underlie the Book's Strategies

Throughout this book, I share the wisdom of educational experts. You will find brief biographies of each of these individuals in the appendix.

Through my own teaching experience, research, and related scholarship in the field of teacher education, I've developed key ideas that position teachers as continuously reflective and intentional learners. These ideas, which follow, serve as the frame for this book. Think of them as my viewpoint or perspective.

Developing Teacher Expertise

There are three main types of teaching expertise that you can begin to develop during the student teaching practicum and build on throughout your teaching career: growth competence, adaptive teaching expertise, and collaborative expertise (Soslau and Alexander 2021; Soslau et al. 2019).

Growth competence is your ability to learn how to learn and to engage in critical reflection before, during, and after instructional delivery for the purpose of continuous professional self-improvement. Support for your critical reflection is woven throughout the book. Teaching experience alone will not enable you to grow your skills; rather *reflection on teaching* is what enables you to engage in continuous learning and improvement now and for years to come.

For example, every teacher can recall a time when a lesson did not unfold the way they had planned. How does a teacher reflect on the lesson in a way that leads to better instructional decision-making? Teachers who have multiple strategies to assess their own lesson effectiveness are practicing growth competence. Teachers might decide to record their lessons so they can rewatch and identify missed opportunities to improve student learning. Or they might categorize and analyze student work to determine students' misconceptions and tie those misconceptions back to their own instruction—identifying ways they could have slowed down, retaught, or modeled concepts a bit differently. All these self-initiated reflective tasks are examples of growth competence.

Adaptive teaching expertise requires being adept at balancing innovative teaching approaches with pupil learning and social emotional well-being, at questioning what seems routine, and at unearthing overlooked causes of common problems of practice. Teachers with this expertise are able to acknowledge unique classroom dynamics, adapt decision-making based on pupil cues, and make real-time decisions to deviate from planned curriculum and instruction.

A wide array of strategies in this text support your growth as an adaptive teaching expert. You will complete activities that help you build connections between students' lived experiences and the required curriculum that you need to teach. Further, you will engage with positive identity development strategies that allow you to create a deeper connection between your instructional decision-making and the social emotional well-being of your students. Through peer observations, you will consider ways to adjust or pivot in order to better engage students.

At some point, for example, every teacher will teach a lesson during which their students become bored, disinterested, or confused. What does a teacher do in the moment they notice this dreaded occurrence? A teacher with adaptive teaching expertise will have the skills first to notice that they are losing their students, and then to reach into their proverbial bag of tricks to select an alternative instructional approach and implement that approach in real time. It is incredibly difficult to notice, sift through alternatives, select one, and implement it in the moment; doing this requires an adaptive skill set honed over time and with systematic, reflective self-assessment.

Likewise, when a teacher wants to stave off a future lack of engagement, they need to be proactive in trying a different instructional approach. Yet this often carries risk. What if the new approach doesn't work? What if students become upset by the change of course? These are risks an adaptive teacher needs to balance. The teacher might explicitly explain their decision-making, they might get parents and guardians on board first, or they might involve their own students in deciding on the best approach to an academic topic. Adaptive expertise is required to implement any of these choices.

Collaborative expertise includes speaking up, speaking out, asking questions, contributing ideas, being vulnerable, and being willing to seek help. In addition to strategies and activities to support your process of building collaborative expertise, you will encounter a range of information to support your growth as a collaborator. In the book, principals offer suggestions about building school-based professional relationships. Practicing teachers share their experiences of partnering with other teachers and of placing love and care at the heart of their teaching. You will also find exercises and sentence starters for productively engaging in difficult conversations as well as ideas and tools to help you build lasting relationships with your students and their families.

Schools can be contentious spaces. Principals may make requests that you deem unreasonable. Colleagues may make inappropriate comments about students. Grade team partners may push back when you attempt to implement an alternative approach to teaching your subject material. These are all people you must be able to work with and, on many occasions, collaborate with for the benefit of your students. So how does a teacher with collaborative expertise reply to the principal? How do they respond to colleagues when they overhear them making disparaging remarks about students? What does a teacher say to defend their curriculum approach and to invite other teachers to explore new avenues to better reach and include students? Collaborative expertise is the set of skills that a teacher uses to navigate these difficult scenarios.

Positioning Yourself as a Teacher and Learner

For you to develop these skills, you need to engage in deep reflection to create or identify opportunities for your own learning and professional development. You also need to be vigilant in keeping the learning of all students foremost in your actions and decisions. Three conditions, when recognized and embraced, will enable you to do this (Soslau and Alexander 2021; Soslau et al. 2019). The following are the conditions:

Embodiment of dual roles. You must see yourself as a teacher of learners *and* a learner of teaching. The fluid movement between these two roles necessitates a willingness to listen to, learn from, and share ideas to improve teaching practice and positively impact pupil learning and well-being.

Positioning, power, and agency building. It's crucial to recognize that you hold a position of power. That is, you are well equipped with innovative coursework and prepared to serve as a classroom contributor on day one of your career. A strong sense of efficacy—the belief that you can positively impact pupil learning and well-being—is essential so you can contribute and thrive as a teacher-learner now and in the future.

Focusing on student learning. The heart of teaching is your impact on young people. You must move beyond your own needs and maintain a vigilant focus on student learning. What do you want students to learn? How will you know if students learned anything? What evidence demonstrates that your decision-making had the desired impact? And what does the student data (anecdotal evidence) mean for your future decision-making (acceleration or remediation)?

These three types of expertise and the three necessary learning conditions anchor this book. My hope is that you will clearly see how each chapter, activity, exercise, and journal prompt supports your development of teaching expertise and enables you to collaborate with various school stakeholders to co-create a learning experience that benefits everyone.

Two Common Truths

Finally, there are two common truths about teaching and learning to keep foremost in mind:

Humans have the capacity to learn and do better.

- All children can learn.
- All teachers can innovate and improve their practice.

Humans do not seek out failure.

- All children want to be successful.
- All teachers want to be successful.

There will be times when your belief in these truths will be shaken. Remember, no one wakes up in the morning, looks in the mirror, and says, "How can I fail today?" No matter what you witness or experience in the classroom or school, always know in your core that with the right mix of effort, support, and resources, we *all* can learn.

1

Getting Your House in Order

Strategies for School Year Preparation

This chapter is designed to prepare you to enter your classroom with concrete ideas to set your students and yourself on a pathway to success. Through questionnaires, letter writing, activities, and discussion, you will gain information about the skills and wisdom your students bring with them to your classroom and plan ways to integrate these skills into the curriculum. You will also request, analyze, and reflect on input from your students' parents or guardians about their expectations and help students develop plans for achieving goals aligned with their families' expectations. At the conclusion of this chapter, you will be able to answer the following questions:

- What are my students' funds of knowledge—unique lived experiences and skills—and how can I connect these skills to the curriculum that I need to teach?
- What community assets are available to enhance my instruction and support my students and their families?
- What expectations do my students' families hold?
- How can I help my students prepare to meet their own and their families' expectations?

Whether they're a teacher candidate, a first-year teacher, or a veteran, all educators need to prepare for the school year by getting to know the community they will serve. The activities in this chapter will help you learn about your students, their families, and the community assets and educational resources that are available to you. You can use this information in your teaching to create contexts for learning that relate to your students' lived experiences—to build connections between students' prior knowledge and the new curricular content you're responsible for teaching. You can use students' unique cultural knowledge as valid curriculum material and processes for learning activities and assessments. The chapter can also support you in figuring out ways to incorporate community assets into your instructional planning and to be responsive to parents' expectations.

Strategy 1: Unearth Students' Funds of Knowledge

Your students arrive at school with specialized skills and experiences. Luis Moll's (2019) concept of *funds of knowledge* includes special skills, expertise, or knowledge that children have developed outside of the traditional school setting (at home, in faith communities, after school, with youth groups, on sports teams, and so on). Funds of knowledge are culturally developed over time, and these learned experiences enable children to contribute to their family and sustain themselves. Many of these types of knowledge and skills are likely to remain invisible to teachers unless students have the opportunity to reveal them.

Learning about and calling on students' funds of knowledge allows you to build connections between students' prior knowledge and the typical curriculum topics and materials. It can help you identify new culturally significant topics of study. You can also incorporate into projects, activities, assignments, and assessments the culturally specific ways students learn and demonstrate understanding.

At the start of each school year, I highly encourage you to find space for unearthing and calling upon students' funds of knowledge. Having students share information through a questionnaire is an efficient way to begin to do this.

Student Questionnaire

The "All About Me: Special Skills and Interests" questionnaire (page 26) is designed to help you elicit information about your students so that you can design a learning climate that builds bridges between their existing cultural knowledge and your required curriculum. In addition to bridging between prior knowledge and new material, you can use students' funds of knowledge as valid learning material and processes for everyone in the classroom, as shown in figure 1.1. With this activity you are working as an educational ethnographer to try to reveal, identify, and uncover the skills, expertise, and knowledge students have gained outside of school. The amount of autonomy you have to do this will vary depending on the grade level you teach, the type of school you are in, your district curricula requirements, your level of principal or administrative support, and the sociopolitical climate where you teach.

Use the questionnaire form in the way that works best with your students and in your setting. Feel free to adapt the form and its questions to the ages and instructional levels of your students and the parameters set by your school and district.

When You're the New Teacher

With younger students or those who have difficulty writing responses, conduct oral interviews and record students' answers. If you have students in the early grades, you might use morning meetings to learn more about students, using chart paper or your own log to note what children share.

As a middle or high school teacher, you might take advantage of advisory periods or electives to find pockets of time. Allow at least 45 minutes for students to complete the questionnaire. If you decide to use it as an oral interview or with the class as a group, plan for two class periods. Your goal is to learn as much as you can about students as individuals so you can make their learning relevant.

If you have large grade rosters of older students, invite students to anonymously input their responses into a shared document using Google Docs or a similar platform. Then students—as opposed to you, the teacher—can collaboratively analyze the responses and suggest curriculum connections and cultural enhancements. This adaptation works especially well in the upper middle and high school levels.

Teacher Reflection and Connection

Once your students have completed the questionnaire, or you've conducted interviews or group discussions, you'll need to reflect on your students' responses. The goal here is to identify students' prior skills or pockets of knowledge that you can incorporate into your instructional plans.

Figure 1.1 Fifth Grade Funds of Knowledge Reflection Chart

Skills and Knowledge	Required Curricular Components	Plan for Curriculum Connections and Cultural Enhancements
Multilingual	Literacy (multicultural texts)	Select multilingual texts that reflect your students' language diversity. Students can help translate and pronounce words, discuss origin of cultural items in text, or draw connections to home life and heritage.
Baking	Mathematics (measurements)	Use manipulatives for measuring units that make use of known items such as flour, oil, or sugar. Have students with baking skills teach how to measure ingredients. Contextualize lessons using baking scenarios. Use a baking activity as a unit review.
Budgeting	Economics (simple budgeting)	Students create a class list of new supplies for an upcoming project. Students with budgeting knowledge lead a mini-lesson on what a budget is and how it can be useful for making financial decisions. Students are given a budget to determine which supplies can be purchased.
Sewing	Social Studies (family culture)	After unit on family structures, students create fabric squares to represent their family crest. Students with sewing expertise model sewing skills. Sewing a classroom family quilt serves as a unit final.
Farming	Science (hydroponics and food source cycles)	Invite family members in to discuss farming. Students with farming expertise can lead a discussion on food cycle sources. Introduce hydroponics and other alternative approaches to traditional farming.

Chapter 1: Getting Your House in Order

Your first step is to read through all responses and make a list of skills and knowledge your students bring to the classroom. You might notice skills such as cooking, meal planning, time management, money management, babysitting, and so on. Using the "Funds of Knowledge Reflection Chart" (page 27), you can begin to think through how you might bridge and enhance your curriculum with what your students already know and can do. A sample chart for an upper elementary school classroom is shared in figure 1.1.

Strategy 2: Discover Community Assets

The community beyond the school is a rich educational source of people, places, and organizations that teachers can use to enhance their curriculum. When teachers connect students with their community in meaningful ways, learning is more engaging and authentic. The purpose of this activity is to identify and plan ways to access these community assets. While it's an exercise that takes extra time, it can also yield rewards, enriching teaching and learning in a variety of ways.

Consider beginning this work a few weeks before the school year starts; though helpful, it's not necessary for you to meet your students or to engage with parents beforehand. Once the school year has begun, it is unlikely you will have a large amount of uninterrupted time to complete this activity. In that case, take 15 minutes each day (perhaps during your prep period) to work through it. The reflection and subsequent planning can be completed at your own pace, as this will become a resource that you can make use of throughout the school year.

Mapping Resources and Gathering Information

Begin by conducting an internet-based scavenger hunt to locate information about resources (such as youth activities, museums, libraries, and businesses) in your local community.

Research and map your findings. Visit neighborhood, city, county, and regional websites that provide information about services, organizations, programs, nonprofits, and businesses to determine what types of resources are available to your students and their families. You might find it helpful to visit the website for your local chamber of commerce and your local library, both of which often provide links to free services and programming for youth. When searching online, try using "youth" as a key word followed by "community centers," "civic organizations," "outreach," and "recreation." Once you locate a list of community resources, you can use the "Concentric Map of Community Assets" form (page 28) to create a visual depiction of the resources that are available to you, your students, and their families. Figure 1.2 is an example of a concentric circle map.

Figure 1.2 Concentric Map of Community Assets

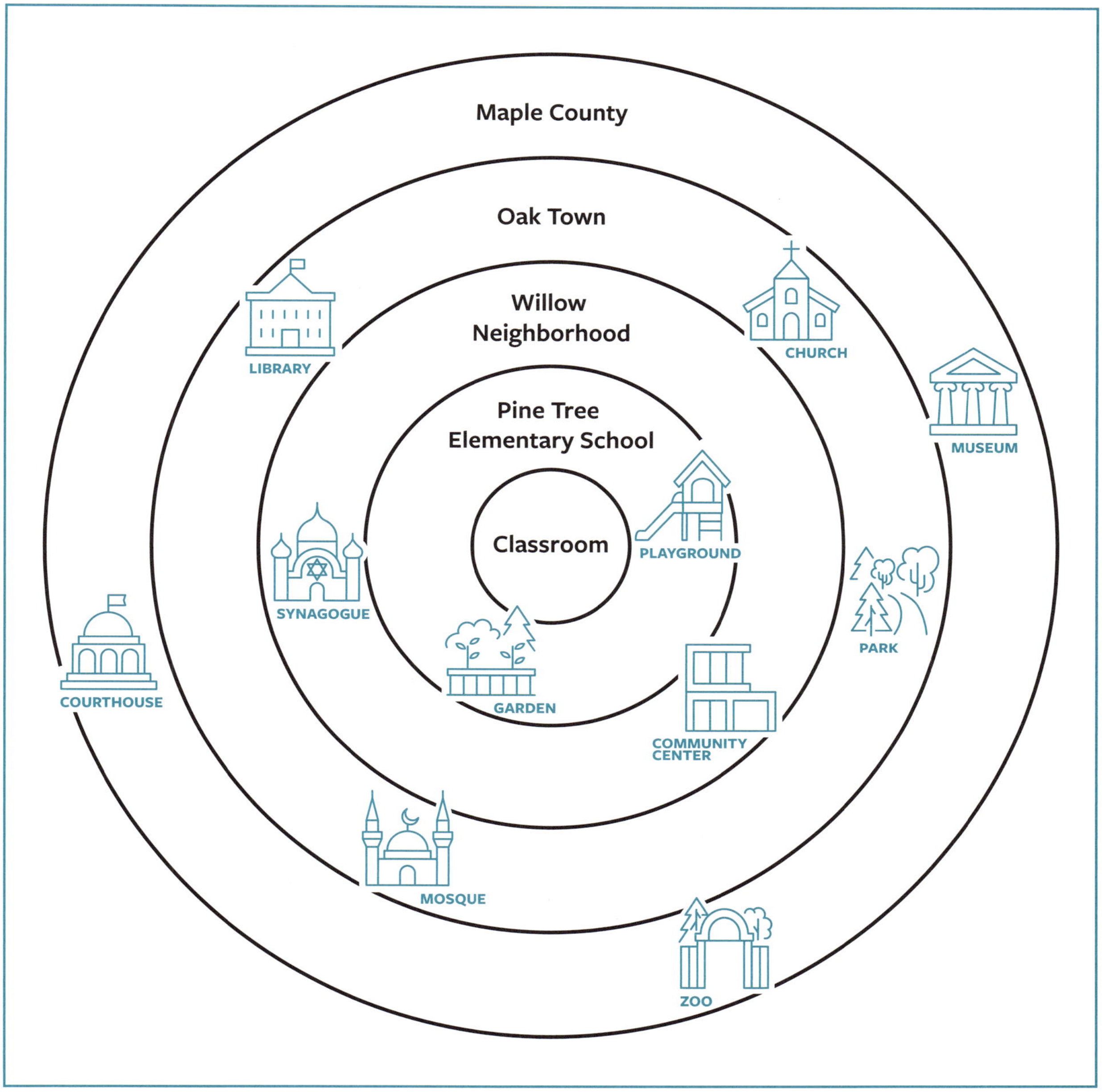

The circles in the figure start with the classroom and span out to include the school, neighborhood, town, and county. The students who attend Pine Tree Elementary School have access to a variety of community resources including a courthouse, a library, a museum, places of worship, a community center, a zoo, and a park. On the school grounds are a garden and a playground.

Reach out for information. Next, contact locations to determine what types of programming are available to children in the community. Be sure to begin your initial contact with a clear introduction to who you are and the purpose of your call or email. For example, "Hello, my name is Elizabeth Soslau, and I'm a fifth grade teacher at Pine Tree Elementary School. I'm calling/emailing to find out what programs you offer for school-age children." Use the "Community Asset Planning" form (page 29) to note any key information you learn. The following questions can help guide your inquiry:

- What programs are offered on site? What are their costs?
- Do you visit classrooms? If so, what types of presentations or assemblies do you provide?
- Are there community experts within your organization who might be willing to teach a lesson or visit my classroom to talk with my students about particular topics?
- I am teaching a unit on . . . Is there anyone at your organization who might be able to co-teach the lesson with me?
- I am teaching a unit on . . . Are there any materials or resources related to our topic that you could lend to my students to explore?
- Does your organization welcome class trips? What types of activities would my students be able to engage in while on site?

Teacher Reflection and Planning

Once you've completed your research, reflect on how you might tap the community resources to support your students' learning and social emotional well-being. Continue using the "Community Asset Planning" form to track your reflection and plan for next steps. In figure 1.3, the first row is completed as an example showing that the teacher has learned about the public library's program, "Read a Dog a Story." Each Wednesday the library can bring volunteer dogs to the school and children can sign up to read to the dogs. The time slot of 11:00–1:30 corresponds with the lunch window for students.

Figure 1.3 Community Asset Planning

Community Asset	Contact Information	Information Discussed	Next Steps
Public Library	Librarian– 215-555-1234	• Library has a "Read a Dog a Story" program where they bring dogs to elementary classrooms. • Wednesdays 11:00 a.m.–1:30 p.m., 15-minute time slots. • For reluctant readers.	• Discuss with principal. • Identify students who may benefit. • Schedule visits from library dogs.

Strategy 3: Identify Family Expectations

Most teachers hold some preliminary ideas and predictions about what families expect to happen at school. However, these assumptions are often inaccurate and may be influenced by biases about students and their families. Each family is unique and will hold a variety of expectations about their child's learning experiences and outcomes—and different families may express their expectations in different ways. It's important that you learn about families' actual expectations so that you can clearly communicate the ways you are planning to meet them.

> ## Talking About Families
>
> Students come from a variety of family arrangements. This book uses the terms *parents, guardians, family adults,* and *families* interchangeably to refer to the adults who live with and care for the children you teach.

The strategies you'll use to do this, explained in detail over the next few pages, include:

- distributing and analyzing a "Family Expectations Questionnaire" (page 30)
- writing a follow-up letter to families to explain how you will address their expectations
- having students interview family adults about their expectations for their child's school experience
- helping students consider their families' and their own priorities and set goals toward meeting them

If possible, send home the family questionnaire at the very start of the school year and then take the following two weeks to collect the responses as parents return their forms. Ideally, you will send your follow-up letter by the end of the first month of school.

Family Questionnaire

With the "Family Expectations Questionnaire," you will open the lines of communication with parents and guardians and establish parameters about how to be in touch. Answers to the questions on the form can help you clarify parents' expectations and give you insight into their priorities and desires—insights that you can use to shape the learning environment and plan instruction and support for students.

You may decide to send the questionnaire home with students, email it to families, or call parents individually to ask the questions. Free translation services for reproducing the questionnaire in families' home languages are often available in school districts. If these services are not available, you might decide to use an online translation service. You might also consider partnering with multilingual teachers, counselors, or even students. There are also free translation apps that enable you to call a parent and have your spoken words translated into their home language. Google Translate is a free service that can be used for both written and audio translation.

Chapter 1: Getting Your House in Order   **15**

You might find it difficult to reach some parents or family members. In this case, consider having students interview their parents. You could assign one question or category per night and have the questionnaire completed in one week. Your reflection time and information analysis can be completed during your prep time (which should take about two prep periods, or longer depending on how many students are on your roster).

Another option is to enlist older students to get involved and help you. Students can follow the six question stages beginning on page 17, and then you can use their analysis to write your parent letter.

Regardless of the approach you use, it is essential you deliberately and systematically reach out to parents and express your desire to learn more, support strong communication, be a partner, or simply keep families informed according to their wishes. Working with parents, at an engagement level *they* deem useful, is a critical component of supporting each child in your classroom.

In some cases, families might hold expectations that you cannot fulfill. In these instances, reaching out for support from your administration and other school personnel, such as a guidance counselor, department chair, or grade team leader, will be useful to you.

TEACHER SPOTLIGHT

Reaching Out to Parents

"Reaching out can be daunting! I find that having open and clear communication with parents about both positive and negative events is the key to overall communication. Parents want to be heard and appreciated."

• • •

"I only speak English and most of my students and their families over the years have not spoken English. This made engaging with families challenging at times, but it has pushed me to grow my Spanish language ability as well as my collaboration with others who have been able to help with translation—not to mention all of the opportunities I've had to grow in cultural competencies."

Analysis of Responses from Family Adults

It is important to take stock and reflect on the information you collect from parents. Look across all the responses to the questions on the form to categorize the results into themes or buckets. Condensing the information in this way will help you make sense of parents' expectations so that you can implement instructional practices and classroom management approaches that help you address family priorities and desires. You can do this efficiently by working in stages, one question at a time.

Question 1

Read all the responses to the first question about children's feelings. Make a list of feelings that parents reported wanting their children to experience during their time in your classroom. Try using a tally mark system to indicate duplicate responses. You may have to collapse words that are similar. Figure 1.4 shows an example of what this might look like.

Figure 1.4 Student Feelings Tally

Now, look at your chart and determine the rank order of feelings based on frequency of parents' reported wishes. Based on the tally in figure 1.4, the ranking would look like this:

1. safe (10)
2. challenged, excited, encouraged (9 each)
3. happy (7)
4. curious, loved (6 each)
5. belonging (5)
6. heard (4)
7. calm (3)

Question 2

Read all the responses to the second question about necessary learning supports to address students' challenges and acceleration needs. Make a student-specific chart to record challenges or acceleration needs and expected supports. If more than one parent reports similar needs, list multiple children in a single cell. Figure 1.5 shows an example.

Figure 1.5 Parent-Reported Student Challenges/Areas of Acceleration and Expected Supports

Student	Challenge/Acceleration	Expected Support
Anali, Cyrus, Emma C.	Math facts	Small group tutoring after-school
Demetrius, Franco, Lily, Rashan	Reading comprehension	Pull-out support from reading specialist
Ezra D., George, Tara	Attention/off task	Keep students on task
Deshaun, Marika, Terri	Reading 2 years above grade level	Provide accelerated texts for reading group
Adrianne, Malcolm, Sandra	Math performance 1 year above grade level	Accelerated math placement for math class

Question 3

Next, read all responses to question 3 about children's special interests or talents and how parents expect their child to develop and build on those interests. Make note of any interests that fall *outside the scope* of the standard curriculum or of accelerations noted for question 2. You may end up with a list of interests/talents that looks something like this:

1. sports
2. music/instruments
3. coding
4. drama/theater/comedy
5. cooking

Question 4

Look at parents' responses about homework quantity and whether their child will be expected to complete homework independently. Note which students will not have homework help available to them after school. Make a list of these students.

Then read through parents' expectations about the quantity of homework. Indicate which parents' expectations are mismatched with your own plans for assigning homework. Your notes might look something like this:

Students without homework help:
- Emma C.
- George
- Liliana
- Nils
- Rashan

Students with parents who expect more homework than planned:

- Deshaun
- Kenta
- Terri
- Vincent

Students with parents who expect less or no homework:

- Adrianne
- Cyrus
- Ezra D.
- Leon
- Tami

Question 5

Now, create a communication chart that aligns with parents' reported preferences for how to keep in touch. The "Family Communication Preferences Chart" form (page 33) can help you do this. Figure 1.6 shows an example of what a few entries on your chart might look like.

Figure 1.6 Family Communication Preferences Chart

Student Name	Parent/Guardian	Phone	Email	Letter	Conference
Garcia, Timothy	Jessica Garcia	✔	✔		✔
Ho, Evelyn	Jonathon Ho	✔			✔
McKenna, Tami	Carla West Mark McKenna	✔	✔	✔	✔
Raduenz, Vincent	Alyssa Raduenz	✔			

Question 6

Next, read the open responses to the final question. Use this feedback from families to augment your previous charts and notes. You might unearth new feelings that were not recorded before or other parental expectations that need to be added to one of the charts above. Be sure to keep note of any additional expectations or requests that do not fit on the charts so that you can reach out to parents individually with your plan to address these concerns.

Once you have organized parents' responses into tables and charts, develop a plan to address these expectations and share your plan with your students' families. Take some time to reflect on all available information. It might be helpful to spread your notes and charts out in front of you, so you have the full picture in mind.

Chapter 1: Getting Your House in Order

Following Up with Families

After taking time to review and reflect on your analysis of the questionnaire responses, draft a letter to send to all students' families to explain how you plan to address the expectations they have shared. Crafting this will take some thought. It's best to keep the letter as brief as possible while doing your best to account for all the information you collected and to address the majority of family expectations in one way or another. If writing a letter feels daunting, or you're not sure if parents will read the letter, an alternative is to create talking points for back-to-school night or other parent events. Figure 1.7 shows an example of a letter.

Figure 1.7 Family Follow-Up Letter

Dear Parent/Guardian,

Thank you so much for taking the time to complete the questionnaire about your expectations for this school year. I learned a lot about what you want your child to experience while in my classroom. Below is my plan for addressing your expectations.

I will:

- follow all school safety protocols, and teach your child personal safety expectations (walk don't run, hands to yourselves, and so on)
- implement the school's social emotional learning curriculum
- invite students to share their feelings and have their concerns addressed
- accommodate your child's learning needs by modifying and adapting the reading and mathematics instruction and assignments
- provide free choice in reading materials and math centers that engage students in a variety of ways
- provide free math tutoring after school on Tuesdays and Thursdays, 3:00 p.m.–3:35 p.m.

Homework policy: Math and reading homework will be assigned Monday through Thursday. Homework is meant to be completed within 30 minutes. You may stop your child after 30 minutes even if the homework is not complete. There is no penalty for incomplete homework. If your child gives their best effort for 30 minutes, their subject grade will not be affected. Of course, if your child wants to complete the homework and work beyond the required 30 minutes, that is fine too!

Parent volunteers: The children in this class have a lot of talents and interests in activities such as sports, cooking, coding, drama, and more! If you are interested in partnering with me on a special activity or lesson related to your child's interests, please let me know.

Open communication: There are several scheduled opportunities to meet with me to discuss the curriculum and your child's progress, including Back to School Night and parent/teacher conferences. I also welcome you to contact me at any time for any reason. You can reach me by email or by calling the school and leaving me a voicemail.

Thank you again for sharing your expectations about this school year with me. I'm looking forward to building our partnership so that we can help your child have a successful year!

Sincerely,
Elizabeth Soslau
5th Grade Teacher

Strategy 4: Help Students Learn Family Expectations and Set Goals

It is important that students understand their parents' expectations of them, and it is useful for students to relay these expectations back to you. With this activity, each student will conduct an interview with a parent, guardian, or another important family adult or family friend to learn about their family's expectations for the school year. Students will plan the questions they will ask, and they can record the interviews (if adults agree to this) or write notes to keep track of responses. Students will then share some of these responses with you and the class in a group activity.

It's best if students pose only a few questions. In this way you respect busy families and make it viable for students to keep track of responses. When introducing this activity to your students, make it clear that the person they interview can be any adult that they live with, or any adult who has their best interest in mind. In my classroom, we called these folks "treasured adults."

Preparing Students to Interview a Treasured Adult

To help students plan their own questions, talk together about the reasons for the interviews. Begin by explaining the activity. You might say: "Today we are going to talk about a way you can learn what your treasured adult expects of you as a student this school year. One way to find this out is to ask them questions. Together we are going to come up with ideas for questions you might ask your treasured adult. The purpose of the interview is to help the two of you figure out goals and actions to help you do well at school. I predict that this interview might be fun because you get to discover your treasured adult's invisible thoughts about their hopes for you as a student."

Chapter 1: Getting Your House in Order

Then discuss questions students might ask, such as the following, inviting students to share ideas and writing them on the board.

- What can I do that would make you feel proud of me this school year?
- How do you expect me to behave in the classroom?
- What can I do to show you that I am working hard and trying my best?
- What skills do you hope I learn this year?
- What do you hope I'll accomplish this year?
- If you had only one goal for me this school year, what would it be? What are your ideas about how I can achieve this goal?
- What kinds of things do you hope to hear about when I tell you about my day at school?

After your discussion, provide copies of the "My Questions for a Treasured Adult" form (page 34). The form has similar questions to the suggested discussion points, shortened and simplified, along with space for students to add their own questions. Explain that the paragraph at the top is for the adult to understand the purpose of the interview.

Student Discussion and Goal Setting

After students complete their interviews, provide an opportunity for them to consider what they learned about their parents' or other treasured adults' expectations. Use the following group activity to help students set goals that align with both their families' and their own priorities and develop some action steps toward achieving them.

1. Set the stage. You might say: "Today we're going to explore what you learned from your interviews with your parents or family grown-ups. At the end of this activity, you will each have developed one goal for yourself, with three steps you can take to reach your goal."

2. Guide students to reflect. Ask them to take a moment to read through their treasured adults' answers. Then say: "Let's hear some responses." Remind students to share only what they're comfortable sharing.

After a few students have commented, read through each question aloud and invite further sharing. Use the following prompts to generate discussion:

- Whose adult said something similar?
- Whose adult said something different?
- What surprised you about what you just heard?
- What is similar or different about what your family expects and what you want?
- How do you wish they had responded to that question?
- How could we take this idea and reword it as an expectation?

22   *When You're the New Teacher*

As students share out loud, record expectations on the board. At the end of sharing, your board might look something like this:

Expectations

Get good grades
Be on task
Read a chapter book
Be a good listener
Do homework
Learn multiplication tables
Be a good friend
Try my best
Give a presentation

3. Guide students to set goals. Now, give each student three to five index cards. Ask them to write one of their family's expectations on each card and spread the cards on their desk.

Then say: "I want you to sort the index cards by importance. For example, if you have three index cards that say 'Be a good friend,' 'Read a chapter book,' and 'Learn multiplication tables,' you will choose the most important expectation and mark it number one. Next, choose and number the second most important expectation, and then the third most important."

Invite a few students to share aloud their most important expectations. Then say: "Now we'll think about how we can turn these expectations into goals."

Chapter 1: Getting Your House in Order

On the board, next to the expectations you listed, write the following sentence starters:

Expectations

Get good grades
Be on task
Read a chapter book
Be a good listener
Do homework
Learn multiplication tables
Be a good friend
Try my best
Give a presentation

Goals

I want to . . .
Steps I can take . . .
I will complete this by . . .
I will know I am successful when . . .
I might need help with . . .
When I reach my goal I will tell my parent . . .

Provide time in class for students to complete their goal-setting plans using the sentence starters. If you wish, students can instead use either the "My Goal for School" form (page 36) or the "Planning and Reaching My Goal" form (page 37). Invite students to ask questions or seek your help as you circulate throughout the classroom to provide support and monitor understanding.

You may decide to have students share their completed goal-setting plans in pairs, small groups, or with the whole class. I suggest that you post students' plans in the classroom. This way the students (and you) can continuously see and be reminded of their individualized goals and plans. Finally, students might enjoy sharing their goal-setting plans with their treasured adults. If this is the case, make a photocopy or PDF of each set of plans before displaying the originals in the classroom.

As an extension, you might consider having students complete another goal-setting activity that may or may not relate to their families' expectations. A wealth of student goal-setting activities are available online for all grade levels. A popular and highly effective approach is to coach students to use the SMART method to set goals that are specific, measurable, achievable, relevant, and time-bound.

• • •

This chapter helped you gather information about your students' funds of knowledge, community assets, and parental expectations. You now have concrete strategies and actions to engage in the following:

- integrating your students' funds of knowledge into your instruction
- making use of community assets to enrich your classroom curriculum
- communicating with families about how you plan to address their expectations
- helping students set and work toward goals that are aligned to their families' expectations

Name: _____ Date: _____

Pronouns: _____

All About Me: Special Skills and Interests

Directions: This form is to help your teacher learn more about you. Answer the questions. Give as many examples as you wish. We will share our answers in class.

1. Outside of school, where do you feel happiest? Why? What do you do in this place?

2. Outside of school, where do you feel most successful or smart? Why? What do you do in this place?

3. How do you spend your time when you're not in school? What do you do?

4. What is the one thing you do best? How did you learn this?

5. If you could teach our class a lesson, what would you teach about? Why?

6. What is something you can do or know a lot about that teachers would be surprised to find out?

Funds of Knowledge Reflection Chart

Skill and Knowledge	Required Curricular Components	Plan for Curriculum Enhancement

Concentric Map of Community Assets

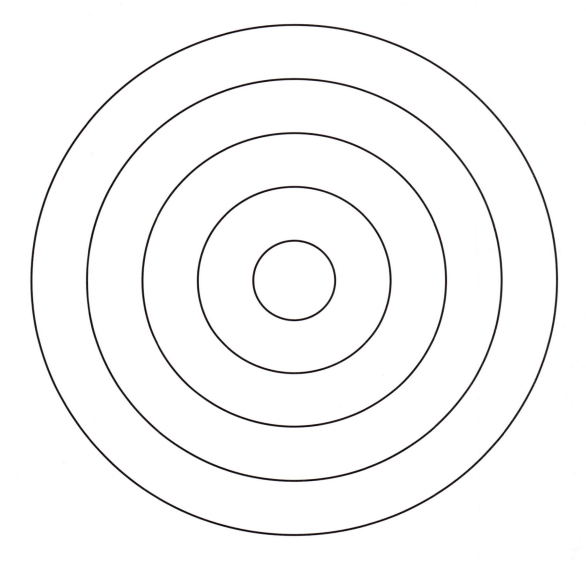

Community Asset Planning

Community Asset	Contact Information	Information Discussed	Next Steps

When You're the New Teacher: 28 Strategies to Align Your Good Intentions with Your Teaching Practices
© Elizabeth Soslau—Free Spirit Publishing

Family Expectations Questionnaire

Dear Parent/Guardian,

This questionnaire is being sent to the parents of all students in my classroom. Please take the time to complete and return it to me by _____.

Answers to the questions can help me understand what your priorities and desires are for your child in the coming school year. Knowing your expectations will help me better understand your child and what you want from their school experience. I will carefully review all responses and send a follow-up letter detailing the ways I plan to address your expectations in my classroom.

Thank you for taking the time to answer these questions.

Sincerely,

Child's name: _____

1. How do you want your child to feel when they are in my classroom?

2. Has your child faced any challenges in school in the past? How were these challenges addressed? How would you like me to address these challenges?

(continued on next page)

(continued from previous page)

3. What special interests or talents does your child have? In what ways do you expect your child to develop and build on these interests and talents?

4. How much homework do you expect your child to receive each night? Do you expect your child to complete their homework independently or will they have access to homework help at home?

5. How would you like me to communicate with you (phone, letters home, email, conferences, and so on)?

6. Please share any other expectations that you have for me or your child.

When You're the New Teacher: 28 Strategies to Align Your Good Intentions with Your Teaching Practices
© Elizabeth Soslau—Free Spirit Publishing

Parent-Reported Student Challenges/ Areas of Acceleration and Expected Supports

Student	Challenge/Acceleration	Expected Support

Family Communication Preferences Chart

Student Name	Parent/Guardian	Phone	Email	Letter	Conference

When You're the New Teacher: 28 Strategies to Align Your Good Intentions with Your Teaching Practices

© Elizabeth Soslau—Free Spirit Publishing

Name: _____   Date: _____

My Questions for a Treasured Adult

About this form: Use this form to interview an adult who cares about you. The purpose of the interview is to help you learn what your treasured adult expects of you at school. It can also help the two of you figure out goals and actions to help you do well in school.

Directions: Ask the questions you want to know about. There is also space for you to write you own questions.

1. What would make you feel proud of me this school year?

2. Describe how you hope I behave in the classroom.

3. What can I do to show you that I am working hard and trying my best?

4. What kinds of things do you hope to hear about when I tell you how my day at school was?

(continued ➜)

When You're the New Teacher: 28 Strategies to Align Your Good Intentions with Your Teaching Practices
© Elizabeth Soslau—Free Spirit Publishing

(*continued*)

5. If you had only one goal for me this school year, what would it be? What are your ideas about how I can achieve this goal?

6. _____

7. _____

8. _____

When You're the New Teacher: 28 Strategies to Align Your Good Intentions with Your Teaching Practices
© Elizabeth Soslau—Free Spirit Publishing

Name: _____ **Date:** _____

My Goal for School

Directions: Write about your goal and your plan to reach it.

My goal is:

This is important to me because:

Steps to reach my goal:

1.

2.

3.

Help I may need:

People who can help me:

When I complete this goal, I will feel:

Name: _____   **Date:** _____

Planning and Reaching My Goal

Directions: Write the steps to reach your goal. Record the date you complete each step and how you feel.

I want to _____

Steps I can take	How I can get help for this step	I plan to complete this step by this date	Actual date completed	How I feel about accomplishing this step

I will know I achieved my goal when:

When I reach my goal, here's what I want to share with my treasured adult and with others:

2

Collaboration Is Essential

Strategies for Building Relationships with Families, Colleagues, and Administrators

Families, teachers, administrators, and students themselves are all stakeholders in children's education. Chapter 3 will take you deeper into strategies for affirming and supporting students. Here in chapter 2, you'll look first at further involving parents in their child's school experience and then at collaborating with other teachers and with your supervising administrators. This chapter will help you answer the following questions:

- What are some strategies I can use to show family adults that I value their partnership?
- In what ways can I build mutually beneficial relationships with my colleagues?
- How can I create a strong working relationship with my principal or other administrators?

Building relationships with parents, colleagues, and administrators is essential for your success at school. The benefits of building strong relationships with families cannot be overstated. Researchers such as Karen Mapp (2003) and Joyce Epstein (et al. 2019) have shown that strong parent-teacher relationships contribute to higher rates of attendance, better homework completion rates, and effective partnerships that support student emotional well-being and academic success. Further, Gloria Ladson-Billings, known for her work on culturally relevant pedagogies, urges teachers to bring families'

39

expertise into the classroom space to create rich cultural contexts for student learning (1995).

When you build relationships with your teacher colleagues, additional opportunities for your own professional growth abound. For example, Robert Marzano (2012) has shown that teachers who collaborate, share resources, and exchange ideas about best practices with their colleagues have more opportunities to innovate and improve their practice. Similarly, interacting with other teachers can expose you to different skill sets. Professional relationships also contribute to feeling more connected to the school community, with many teachers reporting that their colleagues serve as emotional support that helps them deal with the challenges of teaching.

It also behooves you to build a strong working relationship with the administrators in your building, which will pave the way for open communication and trust. Importantly, principals who trust their teachers assume good intent when mistakes are made. Teachers are human. They will be late, they will forget to contact a parent, they will make a poor judgment call when handling a behavior concern. When these mistakes happen, a principal who questions your commitment may reprimand you or take a punitive approach. A principal who trusts that you are working hard to support students and the school community is more likely to approach you with grace.

Beyond this, good relationships with your administrative team will allow you more freedom. Imagine you want to try out a new teaching approach or adjust the suggested curriculum and you approach your principal with your plan. A good relationship will serve as the foundation for a productive conversation about your ideas. And strong trust and communication are bidirectional: the more you trust that your principal has your and your students' best interests in mind, the more likely you are to approach your principal for support when you need advice about how to handle a tricky situation with a parent, student, or colleague or are struggling to understand some aspect of the curriculum.

No teacher can do the hard work of teaching in isolation. Building strong working relationships will ensure that you are not alone in your pursuit of teaching excellence.

Strategy 5: Invite Family Adults to Share Their Expertise with the Class

In the previous chapter, you learned how to connect with families around their expectations and aspirations for their children. In this chapter, you will continue to converse with parents to show that you value their partnership and involvement in your classroom.

Explicitly inviting families to partner with you to support their child's academic success takes some effort, but the rewards can be high. An effective way to get started is by seeking their participation in a specific teaching topic.

Family Expertise Planning Chart

Begin by listing topics that you will be teaching in the coming weeks. Use the "Family Expertise Planning Chart" (page 64) to help you organize the list. This can be a good activity to complete during your lesson planning periods or with your grade team partners. Figure 2.1 shows an example from the form with the first row completed.

Figure 2.1 Family Expertise Planning Chart

Content Area	Topic	Parent/Guardian Involvement
English Language Arts	Students will work on expository text by writing how-to essays. Focus on sequencing and time point words.	Parents can demonstrate tasks and students can then write how-to essays to summarize the steps of the tasks.
Science		
Social Studies		
Mathematics		
Other		

Family Participation Invitation

Draft an invitation to parents inviting them to partner with you on a particular lesson or topic. Your invitation should include the following:

- potential dates
- mode of participation (virtual, in person, video submission)
- length of time
- response options

Figure 2.2 shows an example of an invitation for family participation. It is intentionally brief, and the parent can answer using the same document. Parents are more likely to respond when a teacher's request is clear and easy to reply to.

Figure 2.2 Family Participation Invitation

Dear Parent/Guardian,

This month, your child will write a how-to essay describing the steps to complete a task. We need your help! Think about something you know how to do well; for example, cooking a special dish, home repairs, crafting, and so on. Could you demonstrate this task in person, virtually, or by video so the class can watch and learn?

Please see below and complete this form to indicate your availability. Thank you in advance for sharing your expertise with us!

Sincerely,
Carolina Mendez
4th Grade Teacher

Please circle all options that work for you.

Dates: 10/12   10/13   10/14   10/15   10/16

Time: 9:15 a.m.–9:45 a.m.   9:45 a.m.–10:15 a.m.   2:00 p.m.–2:30 p.m.

Mode: I can present in person.   I can present virtually.

I can submit a 15–20 minute video.

Topic: I would like to demonstrate how to:

Questions: I have a question, please contact me (phone/text or email):

Arranging for Classroom Visits

To organize the volunteer information you received from your students' parents and guardians, return to your planning chart and record the ways in which these classroom visitors will tie into specific curricular areas. Reach out to each volunteer to confirm the date, time, delivery mode, and topic. Be sure to respond to any questions that you receive.

Create a classroom calendar or countdown visual to indicate when visitors will arrive. This visual serves two purposes: it helps keep you organized so you can be well prepared for visitors and it creates excitement as students anticipate welcoming family adults into the classroom.

Strategy 6: Guide Students to Reflect on the Family Visits

After a parent visits your classroom, and before your students write their how-to essays, reflect on the experience with your students. Remember, this activity has a dual aim. First, you are addressing the curriculum-required student task, writing a how-to essay. Second, you are highlighting the importance of family expertise and knowledge as a legitimate aspect of the curriculum. You want students to understand that your required curriculum is only a partial representation of pertinent knowledge and skills.

The following activity will help you show your students that what they learn in their own homes represents valuable and relevant cultural knowledge. Follow these five steps:

1. Review the task that was shared by a family adult.
2. Ask students why this task is important.
3. Ask students to share any cultural significance of the task.
4. Ask students to share how their observation of the family adult will be useful to their own writing process when they begin to write their how-to essay. If students struggle to answer, ask them to think whether and why it would be difficult to write a how-to essay without a live model of someone completing a task.
5. Close by asking students to share other ways they would like parents or guardians to take on the role of content expert and teacher in the classroom.

The following is an example of using these steps in a reflective conversation with fourth grade students.

Teacher: Yesterday, we watched a video of Ms. Oliveras making her family's rice and bean dish. I know I learned a lot. Take a moment to think about what you learned. (*pause*) Now, turn to a partner to share one thing that you learned. (*pause*) Now let's share aloud what you learned.

Student A: I learned that you have to soak the beans for a long time.

Student B: I learned that Ms. Oliveras learned how to make the dish by watching her grandmother.

Student C: I learned that rice and beans is a popular dish all over the world, not just in Puerto Rico.

Teacher: Why do you think it's important to learn how to cook delicious dishes like rice and beans?

Student D: It's important because you have to feed yourself and when you get older you need to feed your family.

Chapter 2: Collaboration Is Essential

Student E: Yes, and you can learn how to cook things that your grandparents and parents cook, so it's a tradition.

Teacher: That's a great point. Why do you think it is important to learn about traditions?

Student F: Well, you can learn about your family and learn about why you cook with certain ingredients. You might learn about where the ingredients come from and why they're good to cook with. And you might learn that certain foods mean something, like a symbol, or like part of celebrations.

Teacher: Yes. You shared two important ideas. Where food comes from can also tell us about agriculture and geography. For example, if people live near an ocean, they might eat different things compared to people who live near fields. Second, people eat certain foods, prepared in certain ways, for special days and holidays or for special reasons. Food and traditions are part of culture, just like language, the way someone dresses, what they value, and even how people see the world. How do you think it would be different if we wrote our how-to essays without inviting family members to share how they complete different tasks—like cooking rice and beans?

Student G: Well, it would be harder to get started. I wouldn't know what to write about. Also, it helps you keep track of steps. Each tiny direction is important. There are a lot!

Student H: Right, and we wouldn't have learned all the stuff that the different parents showed us. Like last week, Tariq's dad showed us the different ways to sew buttons on different types of fabric.

Teacher: Excellent examples. I wonder if you can think of any other ways that your parents could get involved in helping us learn? Take a moment to brainstorm with your table groups different ways parents might become teachers for us.

As an extension of this reflective conversation, students could write their own thank-you notes to parents detailing what they learned from the parent visit. To involve students further, have them draft future invitations and deliver them to family adults themselves.

TEACHER SPOTLIGHT

Parents as Teachers

"When I was a third grade teacher, I taught at a predominately Black charter school. Most of the families were Black, as I am. One day, a student's mother was picking up her child from after-school care. She stopped by my classroom to say hi and chitchat.

"During our conversation, I mentioned that the Black History Month assembly was occurring the next week. The mother asked me what we had planned for the program.

I told her there was a performance planned and, in addition, we were learning about notable Black figures in our city, Milwaukee. This mother responded that we should do more. She explained that the students often learn about typical notable Black figures every February and suggested highlighting lesser-known notable people.

"I said that sounded like a great idea and asked if she could co-plan and co-teach about some of these people with me. That weekend we met at a coffee shop and created a PowerPoint complete with videos, music, and pictures of notable Black figures who might be less known to students. Early the next week, we spoke on the phone to review our slideshow and designate speaking parts. The day of the program, this mother came into the classroom an hour before the assembly and co-taught the lesson with me. The students were so excited and engaged. It was a great 'pre-show' to the Black History Month all-school assembly."

Strategy 7: Use a Four-Step Framework to Navigate Teacher-Family Communications

What parents and guardians want for their children and what they expect of you will vary from family to family. Not all exchanges and communication attempts will go smoothly, yet a smoother process is more likely when you are prepared to manage any difficulties that arise in critical conversations with parents. The following framework can help you build positive relationships and respond to parents who may pose challenges to you.

1. Express gratitude and grace.

- "Thank you for bringing this concern."
- "I hear that you are upset, and I appreciate you sharing this."
- "It is so great that you brought this up because . . ."
- "I can tell you care a lot about this issue."

2. Demonstrate that you are listening.

- "This is important to me; do you mind if I take some notes?"
- "Would it be okay to include the principal in this conversation? It's important for them to hear."
- "I hear you say . . ."
- "Do you mean . . . ?"
- "Can you tell me more about your concern?"

3. Consider delaying a response if necessary.

- "I need some time to digest what you shared. I will circle back to you on . . ."

- "I need to talk about this with my principal/co-teacher/counselor. When would be a good time to get back to you?"
- "These are important concerns—let me conduct a little research. Then I'll share what I learn with you."
- "I need to gather more information from the students, other parents, and school administrators. You can expect to hear from me by . . ."

4. Respond and follow up.

- "Based on what you shared, I plan to . . ."
- "I will address your concerns by . . ."
- "I plan to meet your request by . . ."
- "While I understand your sentiments, I am required to . . ."
- "I will share your concerns with . . ."

The following scenarios show examples of using the framework in a phone conversation and via email.

Scenario 1

A parent disagrees with the inclusion in the classroom library of a book about a family with two dads.

Parent (on the phone): I heard that you are teaching about gay dads in your classroom.

Teacher: I have not taught any lessons about gay dads. I do have a book in my classroom that includes a family with two fathers.

Parent: I don't want my child exposed to a book like that. I need you to remove it immediately.

Teacher: Thank you for bringing this concern to me so that I can address it right away. (*expressing gratitude and grace*) Can you tell me more about your concern related to having the book in the classroom library? (*demonstrating listening*)

Parent: I don't think you should be teaching gay issues in the class.

Teacher: I'm required to have a classroom library that represents a wide array of human diversity and helps all students feel included. Teaching about family diversity is a topic approved by the school administration. I would be happy to share your concerns with my principal—or I can arrange for you to meet with her. (*responding and following up*)

Scenario 2

A parent requests that the unit on Native American history include facts related to boarding schools and the related impact on Indigenous children and their families.

Parent email

Dear Ms. Parker,

Thank you for sharing your curriculum materials with us at Back to School Night. I enjoyed learning more about what Harry will experience this year. I noticed in the social studies textbook that you will be teaching about Native American history this year. I also saw that the textbook describes boarding schools as "places where Indigenous children learned how to be American." As you must know, this is a highly problematic description and incomplete explanation about the true aims of Native American boarding schools. You said you would be supplementing the curriculum in different ways. What are your plans to supplement and adapt the social studies instruction so our children are taught the truth?

Thanks in advance for your prompt reply to this urgent need.
Sincerely,
Sandra Cook (Harry's mom)

Teacher email

Dear Mrs. Cook,

Thank you so much for your careful reading of the social studies textbook. I'm grateful that you brought this issue to my attention. (*expressing gratitude and grace*) I agree that the curriculum needs to be augmented before I teach any lessons about Native American history or about the lives of Indigenous people. I am committed to doing this right. (*demonstrating listening*)

I plan to do some research to identify age-appropriate teaching materials so that I can accurately teach this unit. I will also need to meet with our school's curriculum coach and secure my principal's permission to augment the text. (*delaying response*) I've copied both the principal and curriculum coach on this email, so they are aware of my plans.

I will send you a follow-up email to confirm the outcome of my efforts within the next two weeks. (*responding and following up*) In the meantime, please let me know if you have additional questions or concerns.

In partnership,
Ms. Parker

Strategy 8: Use Peer Observations to Build Partnerships with Colleagues

Cultivating collaborative partnerships with colleagues will enable you to improve your instructional practices and make you a more integrated part of the school community. One approach to help you work toward both these goals is through peer observation practices.

Teachers of all experience levels can benefit from observation feedback. A helpful aspect of peer observations is that they provide a relatively low-pressure way to gain support and fresh perspectives. These observations differ from the evaluative feedback offered by administrators or coaches, because *you* initiate the observation and directly solicit formative feedback from a teaching peer—feedback that is confidential and is not corrective or punitive.

The process of peer observation can be seen as a framework in three stages:

1. **Pre-observation**, where you find a peer observer and meet together to discuss the focus and purpose of the observation
2. **Observation**, where your peer observes you as you teach and notes perceptions and feedback
3. **Post-observation**, where you and your peer observer talk together and you take time to reflect and plan based on the feedback

This section of the book is useful for both you and your observer. You may find it helpful to have pages 49–52 in front of you as you plan together for the peer observation. Follow the process, which walks you through how to identify a peer, conduct observations, and make sense of feedback and suggestions through a reflective activity.

Pre-Observation

Finding a peer observer

Begin by reflecting on the following questions:

1. What are the benefits and drawbacks of selecting a peer in my grade level or in a different grade level?
2. What are the benefits and drawbacks of selecting a peer in my content area or in a different content area?
3. What kind of feedback do I want?
4. Which teachers have the disposition to give me critical and kind feedback?
5. How might I approach a teacher to request that they be my peer observer?
6. What can I offer to my peer observer (reciprocal observation, collaboration on a future project, swapping recess duty, and so on)?

7. What logistical considerations are there (where to sit, use of recording equipment, and so on)?

Once you've reflected on these questions, begin to reach out to your colleagues.

Pre-observation meeting

Before the peer observation session, meet with your colleague to discuss the focus and purpose of the observation. To guide your meeting, draw from these discussion questions:

1. Which aspect of my teaching practice am I hoping to improve?
2. What challenges or problems of practice am I currently facing?
3. What do I hope to get out of the observation feedback?
4. What lesson will I be teaching?
   > What do I want the students to learn?
   > What do they already know about this topic or skill? How do I know?
   > What evidence will I collect from the students to determine if they learned the content?
   > How will I make sense of the evidence?
   > What are possible challenges that might arise during the lesson?
   > What are my plans to address these challenges?
   > Are there students or groups of students who I can predict will have trouble with the lesson?
   > Are there students or groups of students who I can predict will need acceleration during the lesson?
   > What are my plans for supporting those students? How will I differentiate based on students' needs?
5. Logistics: Where do I want the peer observer to sit? How should they take notes? Can they use video or audio recording devices? When will we meet to discuss the feedback?

Conducting the Peer Observation

There are many ways to conduct a lesson observation. A plethora of observation tools are available to you. In my book written with Monique Alexander, *The Comprehensive Guide to Working with Student Teachers*, we recommend twelve different strategies to capture observation data, ranging from pupil competency checklists to traveling maps to content charting. These examples for observing teacher candidates are equally pertinent for peer observations.

One example of an observation note-taking approach we recommend is called *selective verbatim*. In this approach, you first decide on the focus of the observation; perhaps you want your observer to provide feedback on your ability to foster peer-to-peer discussions. The observer will then take notes to capture the exact words you use to encourage student interactions.

Chapter 2: Collaboration Is Essential

A peer observer might also keep a running notation list to track the discourse pattern. For example, each time they hear you ask a question, they write TQ (teacher question). If a student responds, they write SR (student response). If you must give a prompt before another student shares an idea, the observer writes TP (teacher prompt). Each time a student asks a question, the observer writes SQ (student question). The resulting notes might be: TQ, SR, TP, SR, TP, SR, SQ, TP, SR, SR, SR, and so on. With this type of observation note-taking, you will have a record that lets you see how many times you need to prompt students to engage in the discussion.

If your peer has also been able to capture your actual spoken words using selective verbatim, then you can also see which specific spoken prompts seemed most effective in generating student discussion.

You may decide to use a flexible tool based on the goals and purposes of the observation discussed in the pre-observation meeting. Perhaps you want to work on your questioning strategies; in that case, you might ask your peer reviewer to chart all the questions that you ask during the lesson, using the "Peer Observation Form" (page 65). Together you can then analyze the types of questions you used.

Post-Observation

Once the observation is complete, you will meet to discuss the notes, suggestions, and feedback. Following is a sequence with questions to consider when meeting post-observation.

Questions about the lesson from the peer observer

For suggestions and feedback to be useful, the peer observer must fully understand the invisible rationale behind the teacher's decision-making. Observation feedback often includes notations that lead to assumptions. For instance, an observer may notice a teacher circulating throughout the classroom, yet not know the purpose of their movement. Perhaps the teacher is collecting data about students' understanding of content or attempting to identify which students need remediation or acceleration. Alternatively, the teacher could be using proximity control to keep students on task, selecting students who will share out after the activity, or trying to make pacing decisions for the next steps of the lesson.

With so many possibilities, it's important that your peer observer begins by asking questions about the lesson. Sentence starters like the following can help the observer launch your conversation:

1. Can you share your rationale for . . . ?
2. What were you thinking when. . . ?
3. I noticed . . . Can you share a bit about that?
4. When you did . . . I noticed that . . . Is that the outcome you were hoping for?
5. Did you deviate at all from your pre-planned instruction? Why or why not?
6. What else do you want me to know about how the lesson unfolded?

50   *When You're the New Teacher*

Feedback and suggestions from the peer observer

Once all their questions are answered, it will be easier for the observer to give constructive comments and suggestions, within some key parameters.

First, feedback should address only the targeted focus discussed in the pre-observation meeting. For example, if the focus was on the use of higher-order thinking questions, the observer does not give feedback on classroom management, keeping their emphasis on your questioning strategies.

The observer's suggestions also need to be specific and actionable so you will be able to implement them. As an example, "You need to be more engaging" is vague and undefined. Rather, the observer might suggest, "I know you said you want to work more on your discussion approaches. I noticed that your initial questions are highly engaging and elicit a lot of student responses. Let's talk about how to keep students involved for follow-up discussion."

Feedback should be critical but kind and invite the finding of solutions together:

- "You taught a highly complex math concept today and your modeling on the projector was very clear and easy to follow. I noticed that three students in the back of the room were struggling during independent work. Let's think about how you could provide some additional support to these students, perhaps with manipulatives, pulling them into an intervention group, or some other differentiated approach."

- "I noticed that your students were incredibly focused and engaged through-out your lesson. Let's talk about how you could capitalize on your great classroom climate. Perhaps we could think through ways to incorporate some student autonomy through partner work or small groups."

Planning together for continued peer partnership

A single observation, while useful, is insufficient for truly innovating and improving your practice. With your peer observer, discuss questions like the following to continue building your partnership:

1. When will the observed teacher conduct a peer observation of their colleague?
2. Is a follow-up lesson observation warranted? If so, when will it happen?
3. How often do the two of you want to observe each other?
4. Will other teachers be invited to join the peer observation team?

Your reflection on the peer observation process

Finally, take a few moments to reflect on the experience and process of being observed by a peer and to plan next steps. Consider prompts like these:

1. How did it feel being observed by a peer?
2. What were the benefits and challenges of the peer observation process?

3. What is the most important takeaway from the post-observation conference?
4. How will I use the peer feedback to improve or innovate my instructional practice?
5. Which other aspect of my practice do I want to improve? How might the peer observation process support these improvements?

Strategy 9: Form or Join a Teacher Inquiry Group

A highly effective way to collaborate with your colleagues is through a teacher inquiry group. An inquiry group is an opt-in gathering of teachers who agree to meet around particular problems of practice.

Much research is dedicated to examining the many benefits of teacher inquiry groups. The purpose at the heart of an inquiry group is to improve some aspect of schooling. The improvement can be focused on a teacher's own practice, the innovation of an entire grade team, or a cultural and climate objective for the whole school. Teacher inquiry groups may have informal leaders, but they do not include administrators or other authorities outside the rank of teacher. Below is the outline of a process to form an inquiry group.

Forming the Group

Someone (maybe you!) first must decide to form a group. In my own professional experience, this decision happened in conversation with a colleague. We noticed that there were several issues with our teacher preparation curriculum and each problem fell under the broad topic of equity. We wanted to find out if other colleagues felt similarly and, if so, whether they would be interested in helping us form an equity inquiry group. Our focus would be to educate ourselves and work toward the goal of addressing equity-related issues. My colleague and I each spoke to a few other faculty members who agreed to help us form the inquiry group.

Four of us, as a start-up team, approached our administrator and asked her to announce our idea to form an inquiry group focused on addressing issues of equity in our curriculum. Our administrator announced the group at a full faculty meeting, and the start-up team followed up with everyone via email. Our email included a Google poll to gauge folks' interest in joining the group and preferred meeting dates and times. We also invited people to share their own problems of practice, which we framed as dilemmas, focused on equity issues. We used the poll responses to invite willing colleagues to become part of our group.

There are many ways you or your colleagues might go about forming a group. I highly recommend not going it alone. If you identify a problem of practice, talk to other teachers you trust to determine if the issue might be affecting others and if an inquiry group might be useful to engage in collective self-education and problem-solving. Get at least one other person on board before attempting to form a group.

When forming a new group, be sure to send an open invitation. No one should feel mandated to participate, but everyone should feel welcome to do so. One way to extend an invitation is to announce the start of the group during a staff meeting. This way you can fully explain the purpose and focus of the group. Your start-up team can then follow up with an email invitation prior to the first inquiry group meeting.

Figure 2.3 shows an example of an invitation from an equity inquiry group.

Figure 2.3 Inquiry Group Invitation

Hello to all prospective Equity Inquiry Group members,

Thank you so much for responding to the poll about starting an inquiry group! We are pleased that you want to become a group member. Our first meeting will be **November 29, from 10:30 a.m. to 12:00 p.m.,** in room 207.

At the meeting, we will discuss one equity-focused teaching dilemma, or problem of practice, submitted by a member of the group. The teaching dilemma should be related to your own experience teaching or interacting with students. If you're interested in bringing a dilemma to discuss with the group, please use the attached forms to write a description of your dilemma and the questions you wish to resolve. **Email your dilemma to us by November 14.**

The start-up team will choose a dilemma from all submissions to address in the first meeting and will email the dilemma to everyone in the group by November 16 so you have ample time to review it. Our goal is to address all submitted dilemmas over subsequent meetings.

Proposed agenda:

- Explore the selected dilemma (45 minutes). One teacher will share their dilemma. The group will follow a protocol that enables us to listen, understand, and develop some ideas to support the teacher in addressing it.
- 15-minute break
- Further discuss the dilemma as needed and reflect together on ways to refine our inquiry process and hone our equity focus for this school year (30 minutes).

Guiding questions:

As an inquiry group, we need to both support each other and grow together in our understanding of equity issues and ways we can impact them in our school.

Chapter 2: Collaboration Is Essential

Below, we provide some big-picture guiding questions that were developed by the inquiry group start-up team. They reflect the overarching focus and goals of our Equity Inquiry Group. If you have additional inquiry questions, please email us with your questions so your ideas can be addressed during the meeting.

- How do we center issues of equity and justice across our curriculum?
- How do we support one another to do this in our daily work with students?
- How can we incorporate community-based learning experiences and teaching approaches in our curriculum?
- How can we influence school-level structures and systems to prioritize issues of equity and justice?

Thank you for your interest in working together on behalf of your colleagues and students.

Sincerely,

Janna da Pina
Samantha Yang
Surena Robbins
Abe Berkowitz

Setting a Meeting Protocol

Once the group is formed and a meeting focus is set, a protocol needs to be developed to guide the first part of the meeting focused on exploring one teacher's dilemma or problem of practice. A protocol is a set of guidelines the group agrees to use for their conversation. The protocol followed in this chapter is inspired by the early work of Gene Thompson-Grove, Paula Evans, and Faith Dunne of the Coalition of Essential Schools, which was later revised by the National School Reform Faculty's Harmony Education Center. If my reimagined version of the original protocol is not a good fit for your inquiry group, there are many free, open-source protocols available from the National School Reform Faculty's Harmony Education Center (nsrfharmony.org).

Figure 2.4 Summary of a Basic Protocol for a Teacher Inquiry Group

Before the meeting

- Teacher(s) reflects individually to define a problem of practice
- Teacher(s) submits their problem of practice to team leaders
- Team leaders review submissions, select one, and distribute to the full group

During the meeting

- Teacher presents the problem of practice or dilemma
- Group members ask questions (as needed)
- Group members offer discussion, feedback, suggestions
- Presenting teacher mirrors and summarizes ideas and takeaways
- Group members clarify comments (as needed)
- Close with a group reflection on process

Preparing for the Meeting

The protocol described in this chapter and summarized in figure 2.4 is designed for a teacher to present a problem of practice and gather ideas from colleagues about how to address the problem. A problem of practice is a teaching issue or dilemma that is impeding a teacher's success or the success of their students. Any teacher experiencing a dilemma can reflect on a set of questions and then write a concise summary to submit for discussion along with specific questions to ask the inquiry group members. Forms for this purpose, "Reflection on a Problem of Practice: Questions to Consider" and "What's the Dilemma? Summary and Details about a Problem of Practice," are on pages 66–67. The reflection questions and the write-up of the dilemma are then shared with all group members before the meeting, allowing them to also do some preflection about the teacher's dilemma.

Figure 2.5 illustrates a ninth grade teacher's explanation and examples of a problem of practice.

Figure 2.5 Framing a Problem of Practice

My Dilemma

When a student expresses a bias, stereotype, or some other discriminatory statement in class, I don't have enough productive ways to respond that will support that student and the others in the class as well.

Classroom Example 1

During a presentation to a science class

Student: African Americans are more susceptible to heart disease and diabetes.

What I replied: Actually, research shows that race is not a genetic factor that makes people more susceptible to heart disease. People of color are more systematically exposed to stress because of institutionalized racism, which we've talked about before. And stress impacts people's health. These social factors, as well as others, explain higher rates of heart disease for people in some racial groups that are subjected to systemic racism. There isn't a direct relationship between skin color or cultural heritage and heart disease, though.

My questions: Now what? I don't know what to say next, or was this sufficient? Three big questions: (1) How do I find the balance between supporting and guiding the student while also acknowledging and supporting what other students (or myself as the teacher) feel? (2) How do I allow time for growth and reflection when I feel a sense of urgency about how the student or teacher may be offending and hurting other students? (3) How do I engage resistant students (or teachers) without alienating them?

Classroom Example 2

During a class discussion about using nicknames and terms of endearment to improve classroom climate

Student: My math teacher always calls students "brother" and "homie." I'm thinking that this is an example of the teacher trying to relate to her students. Something about it feels phony. What do you think?

Me: I wonder a few things. What makes it feel phony to you?

Student: Well, the teacher is white and white people don't usually talk that way. Especially white adults.

Me: So you are noticing that this teacher is using slang terms that probably don't reflect how she typically talks. Do the students ever use this type of slang to address the teacher?

Student: Yeah, sometimes. But it is still weird and feels wrong.

Me: I think you're right in your original comment. She is trying to relate to her students. But if her students read her as phony, her attempts are not working and may even be hurting students. What do you want to do next? How do you want to address your feelings that your teacher is being phony?

My questions: Was it fair to ask the student how they wanted to handle the next steps? Should I have offered to address the issue with the teacher? Do I share this with the teacher? Was it okay to point out that this teacher might be hurting her students? Should I have pointed out the racial aspect and co-opted use of slang?

Following the Meeting Protocol

Opening (10–15 minutes)

The teacher presents their problem of practice and shares specific real-life stories and anecdotes that illustrate their problem of practice. The sharing ends with posing the cross-cutting questions the teacher hopes the group can address.

Questions (as needed)

The inquiry group members ask questions to resolve any confusion and ward off potential misunderstandings. They may need more context or details to better understand the problem of practice.

Discussion (25–30 minutes)

Here the group discusses the problem of practice while the original presenting teacher listens. This can be difficult for the presenting teacher, but it is essential that they focus on listening to their colleagues. It is highly recommended that the presenting teacher take notes during the discussion. These notes will help the presenting teacher mirror back what they heard as a check for understanding. The group may discuss some or all of the following questions:

- Have any of us, or a teacher we know, faced this problem of practice or one similar? What did we, or they, do?
- What else might the teacher need to know before addressing this problem of practice?
- Which aspects of the problem can be addressed in the short term and which aspects might take longer to address?
- What resources might be available to address this problem?
- Is there a book, article, or other academic reading that might be useful for us to explore to generate ideas?
- What do we think is within, and not within, the teacher's control?
- Are there aspects of the problem that we do not agree are problematic? Which ones and why?
- Are there additional aspects that the presenting teacher did not discuss that we think should be discussed and addressed? If so, what and why?

Presenter summary and mirroring (10 minutes)

The presenting teacher now has time to mirror or restate what they heard, summarizing the key points, questions, and ideas about addressing the problem of practice. Questions like the following can help the teacher frame these ideas:

- What did I hear that resonated most with me? Why?
- What did I hear that was surprising? Why?
- What was the most helpful? Why?
- What did I hear that might signal that the group misunderstands me?
- What questions do I still have?

Chapter 2: Collaboration Is Essential

Clarifying (5–10 minutes as needed)

Based on the mirroring, the inquiry group affirms, clarifies, and adds any missing information that the presenting teacher did not mention.

Group reflection (10 minutes)

The group reflects on the process of the meeting with an eye for improving future meetings:

- What worked well during this meeting and what do we want to keep doing?
- What worked less well and what might we do to improve?
- If we conducted the activity again, what would we do differently? Why?
- What are our hopes for the next meeting when we explore another colleague's dilemma?

Strategy 10: Develop Relationships with Administrators

While building relationships with parents and colleagues is critical to your success, it is also important to build and maintain strong working relationships with your supervisors, principal, and other administrators. Doing this doesn't have to induce anxiety. Though people in these roles often have a good deal of power over your job satisfaction and your employment longevity, you can help shift the balance and claim agency by positioning yourself as a partner.

Positioning Yourself as a Partner

Principals confirm that teachers who build and maintain communication with school leaders reap benefits for students and teachers alike. While writing this book, I spoke with many teachers and principals who affirmed this. Principal Erik Jones noted that these teachers "are more engaged in professional learning opportunities, able to advocate for needs effectively with positive outcomes, and establish positive relationships amongst peers." He went on to say, "The practice of communication is not one sided; both parties are actively involved."

Administrator Jaela Hall-Russell emphasized that "teachers should take initiative and be proactive when building relationships with their administration." Michelle Bernardi, a seasoned Philadelphia middle school teacher, agreed that a positive relationship with your principal is essential and recommended trying to find common ground. "As a special education teacher, I really connected with my principal, who also taught special education. I felt safe to ask for advice and truly supported through all of my struggles."

To set the stage for a productive relationship, it's important that you prioritize engaging early in strong communication with your principal—communication that signals your commitment to your students and to your own professional growth. Though the start of the school year is undoubtedly a busy time for both of you, your efforts to schedule a brief meeting can enable you to set the tone for the school year to come.

So, what does this look like? Where do you start?

1. Request a brief meeting. Send your request via email in the summer or through a phone call. Suggest meeting for 10–15 minutes before or after school. The idea is that you want to get a one-on-one meeting on the books very early in the school year, perhaps even before students arrive for the first day. In your request, state your purpose. For example:

- "I'd like to share some of my professional growth plans with you."
- "I'm seeking some advice about how best to work with you this year."
- "I'm hoping to get some clarity about your expectations of me this year."
- "I'd like some insights about opportunities to get more involved with the community this year."
- "I have a new project idea that I'd like to get your feedback on."

2. Prepare for the meeting. Keep the ultimate purpose of this meeting top of mind: to position yourself as a partner with your principal. During the meeting, ask any questions you might have and share your own ideas about the upcoming school year. While there is a power differential inherent in teacher-principal relationships, remember that you're both there for the same reason. You are both dedicated to providing children with an excellent education.

Make some notes you can refer to during the meeting with key talking points and questions. Be sure to explain how you will be actively involved in whatever topic it is that you decide to broach during your meeting. You want to be able to articulate your goals and build a bond with a short introduction and explanation. Consider these examples:

- "I'd like to share some of my professional growth plans with you. I plan to attend a teaching conference focused on culturally responsive teaching. This is an area of my practice I've been working to improve. Last year I worked to include more multicultural authors in my classroom library. This year I want to gather more insight about my students' life experiences—outside of school—and incorporate these insights into my teaching. Do you have any thoughts or ideas for me as I try to grow in this area? Would it be possible for you to observe one of the lessons that I plan so I can get your feedback?"

- "I'm hoping to get some clarity about your expectations of me this year. I'm so excited to get back to school! Last year, you gave me extensive feedback on my classroom management techniques, and I know that those exchanges were helpful for building a positive climate in my classroom. I'm wondering what expectations you have of me this year. Is there an area of growth that would be beneficial for me to focus on? I want to get a jump start on my own

Chapter 2: Collaboration Is Essential

professional growth plans by checking out some conferences or workshops that would fit with your suggestions."

- "I'd like some insights about opportunities to get involved with the local community this year. In my last semester of school I took a class about community-engaged teaching. It was super exciting, and I want to bring what I learned to my first classroom. I've done some preliminary research and found three nonprofit agencies that partner with schools on different projects. Here's what I learned . . . Do you support my plans? And do you have any additional ideas about how to connect the classroom to the community?"

3. Hold the meeting. Notice, this doesn't say "attend" the meeting. That's deliberate. This is your meeting: you initiated it and you set the agenda. Again, it is important you position yourself as a partner.

Be mindful of time. You asked for a brief meeting. Do your best to stay focused on the topic you selected and do not hesitate to reference your notes throughout the meeting. You want to demonstrate respect for your principal's time by being prepared and adhering to the predetermined time limit. You might open by saying, "I know you're busy, and I appreciate you making the time to meet with me." Then share your key thoughts and questions, allowing room for the principal to interject and dialogue if they wish.

4. Express gratitude. Do this at the end of the meeting and follow up afterward as well. For example: "Thank you so much for meeting with me to collaborate on this idea. Your insights are valuable to me, and I am thankful for your support."

Tips for Responding to Principal Feedback

Your principal or other building administrator will most likely observe your teaching and provide you with feedback about your instructional practice. Some feedback may be critical and hard to hear. However, principal feedback can be valuable since your principal has likely observed many teachers across various content areas and grade levels. This observation experience positions principals to share insights that you otherwise would not have access to. Nevertheless, you might find yourself wondering how to respond to your principal's critical feedback.

1. Pause. You do not need to respond to written feedback right away. Have a trusted colleague read the feedback and ask them how they would respond. Put the feedback away and read it a day or two later. If the feedback is spoken, it's fine to say, "I'd like some time to think about that."

2. Reflect. Consider the feedback. Use the following prompts to help you make notes and process what you've heard.

- How do I feel when I read or hear this feedback?
- What rings true about this feedback?

60   *When You're the New Teacher*

- What rings false about this feedback?
- What steps can I take to address this feedback?
- What follow-up questions do I have about this feedback?
- If I implemented this feedback, how would my teaching change? How would I grow as a professional?

TEACHER SPOTLIGHT

First-Time Observation

"I was observed by my principal with no awareness of the process. She just came into my classroom and sat at a side table for about 20 minutes. At the end of the day, I checked my mailbox and saw a sheet of paper. It was my first observation and there were many positive elements.

"What stood out to me was the comment that I needed to 'cut back on the sarcasm.' I felt stunned. I had no idea what I'd said or done that was sarcastic. I was twenty-six years old at the time and no one had ever told me I was a sarcastic person. So, I asked the principal in a nice way for a little guidance. I explained that I needed to understand what I said that was sarcastic. When she explained my facial reactions and subtle comments, I felt flushed with embarrassment. Honestly, this was the first time in my adult life that the concept of self-awareness started, and I had to take a hard look at my character traits and how my first graders would feel.

"As I talked to family and friends, I realized I needed to adjust my 'in-school personality' for the sake of the students. Ultimately, I grew up quickly and learned the absolute importance of understanding myself and how to show my true care for others."

---

3. Respond. Some principals hold post-observation meetings or request a reflective response from the observed teacher. Use the ideas you drafted in step 2 to prepare for your meeting or written response. Be sure to thank the principal for their time and insights. Share your plans to address the feedback, ask follow-up questions, or speak back to aspects of the feedback that don't fit with your understanding about your own instructional decisions.

Many principals provide feedback based purely on observation. There will undoubtably be instances where the principal will have to guess your internal motivation or rationale for making a particular instructional decision. This is your opportunity to share the insights that they did not have access to during the observation. For example, they might find fault with your decision not to pull a small group for intervention. You might share that you were using this lesson to learn about which students needed either remediation or acceleration and that you have small groups planned for later in the week.

Do's and Don'ts for Building a Positive Relationship with Your Principal

Much of the guidance in this chapter on building relationships with principals came from administrators I've worked with or interviewed for this book. These principals also shared do's and don'ts to help teachers know what works best when communicating and collaborating with them. Here is a summary of their insights, along with ideas from teachers as well.

Do . . .

- Know and keep in mind that your principal wants the best for students and for you.
- Be genuine in your interactions with your principal. Build mutual trust by being respectful and truthful at all times and expecting the same in return.
- Be supportive and be open to trying initiatives and things your principal has planned.
- Be active in extracurricular areas.
- Interact with your principal at least once a day, even just to say "Good morning" or "Have a nice afternoon."
- Use your principal as a resource for instructional and operational needs.
- Be solution oriented when having conversations to solve problems.
- Use the principal as a mentor.
- Advise the principal of issues of concern regarding staff and students.
- Communicate quickly and clearly about emergency situations.

Don't . . .

- Interpret critical feedback as an attack on you. Your principal may be criticizing your pedagogical approach or your decision-making, but they are not criticizing you as a person.
- Oppose or belittle principals publicly (in front of parents, on social media, at a faculty meeting). When you oppose something strongly, do so in person, one on one.
- Be rigid and believe that the thing that has always been done one way has to continue to be done that way.
- Visit your principal *only* with complaints.
- Use a hostile or sarcastic tone or inflammatory language.
- Tell the principal what they *need* to do or *should* have done.
- Provide ultimatums.
- Use the teacher-principal relationship to retrieve confidential information.
- Bring unfounded gossip to the principal.

Reflecting on the Relationship You Want

Take a moment to reflect on what's important to you in your relationship with your principal. Consider ideas like these:

- Words that describe my ideal relationship with my current or future principal are . . .
- Action steps I can take to foster my ideal relationship include . . .
- Questions I wonder about are . . .
- Ways I can unearth answers to my questions include . . .
- My plan to build and maintain a partnership with my principal is . . .

• • •

This chapter helped you learn how to partner with school stakeholders and build relationships to enhance your own and your students' learning experiences. You now have concrete strategies and actions to:

- build positive relationships with parents, colleagues, and principals
- craft ways to engage parents in your classroom
- work with teachers to improve your instructional practices
- maintain strong working relationships with your principal and administrators

Family Expertise Planning Chart

Content Area	Topic	Parent Involvement

Peer Observation Form

Date: _____

Teacher: _____   Peer observer: _____

Goal or focus of observation:

Notes and observations:

Peer observer questions:

Feedback and suggestions:

Reflection on a Problem of Practice: Questions to Consider

Use your journal to reflect on and record your responses to the following questions:
Describe the problem. Why is this a problem? Whom does it affect?

1. Can you share a few anecdotes or real-life examples of this problem? What does it look like "in practice"?
2. Is this problem yours to solve? What's in your control or influence? What isn't?
3. In what ways have you attempted to solve the problem? What were the results?
4. Why do you think the issue has continued to be a problem?
5. What features of the problem concern you most?
6. Do you know other teachers who have faced this problem? What have they done? Why would their approach work/not work for you?
7. What have you read or researched related to your problem? Was this information useful? If so, how? If not, why?
8. What is unique about your problem of practice?
9. In what ways will solving this problem help you and your students?
10. In what ways would discussing this problem be beneficial to other teachers in the inquiry group?
11. What do you hope to learn from inquiry group members when you present your problem?
12. Craft three specific questions you want to ask the teacher inquiry group.

What's the Dilemma? Summary and Details about a Problem of Practice

A problem of practice is a teaching issue or dilemma that is impeding your success or the success of your students. Take some time to reflect on your problem of practice. Then, in writing, clarify your problem so you can readily explain it to colleagues. Describe the problem, give specific examples and actions you have taken, and list what questions you wish to discuss.

My Dilemma:

Classroom Examples:

My Questions:

3

Love and Care in Teaching

Strategies for Affirming Student Identity and Belonging

This chapter explores the role of love and care in the classroom context. It is not often that folks who run professional development workshops or teacher preparation courses talk about love in schooling. Yet, at its heart, good teaching is an act of love. *Care* is the term often used by educational theorists such as Nel Noddings (1984). Other scholars including bell hooks (1994), Bettina Love (2019, 2023), and Gholdy Muhammad (2020, 2023) have extended Noddings' theories of care to explicitly center love in their teaching and encourage others to do the same. In this chapter you'll find answers to the following questions:

- What role do love and care play in the classroom?
- In what ways can I affirm my students' identities?
- How do I build a classroom community?

In chapter 1, you were introduced to setting high expectations for your students through goal-setting activities. Having high expectations and holding students accountable for working hard is an expression of love and care for your students (Ladson-Billings 1995). In this chapter, you will learn to enact practices that communicate to your students that you can be trusted, that you deeply care about who they are, and that you are committed to creating the type of classroom environment that supports their academic *and* emotional well-being. While loving children is no doubt an unteachable orientation to the profession, the act of demonstrating love and care is a set of professional skills and practices that can be learned, rehearsed, and improved over time. This chapter offers activities to support you in cultivating these practices.

Strategy 11: Recognize the Importance of Demonstrating Love and Care for Students

When I ask my preservice teachers why they want to become a teacher, their answer is often, "I want to be a teacher because I love children." Some of my colleagues rebuke this reply as naive, insufficient, corny, and unintellectual. I wholeheartedly disagree. Loving children is an intangible disposition that I cannot teach. Sadly, teacher preparation programs rarely, if ever, include coursework on love and care in the classroom. Yet all students need trusted adults who can affirm their identity, show them they are valued, foster a sense of belonging, identify supportive resources, and lend a listening ear. You, as a teacher, can be one of those trusted, caring adults.

Now, more than ever, love and care are essential pedagogical frames, or ways to think about and orient our teaching approaches. Students' stress and anxiety levels are at an all-time high. In a survey of students from across twenty different U.S. states, researchers found "depression, stress, and anxiety" to be the most frequently reported obstacle to learning in the middle and high school grades (YouthTruth 2022).

Students consistently report that strong relationships with teachers are a key factor to their success in the classroom and to their emotional well-being. Alarmingly, the number of students who report having access to a trusted caring adult who they can talk to drops off after the early elementary grades (YouthTruth 2022). You have the power to disrupt this trend, no matter what grade you teach, and the activities in this chapter can help you.

TEACHER SPOTLIGHT

Love and Care for Students

"My best friend, Kelly, and I went through undergrad together and had daily phone calls during our first years of teaching. In my fourth year on the job, I became her teaching partner. I learned a lot about love and care for students from Kelly. She had a way of helping kids settle and belong by making them her assistant. If she noticed that a kid was having a bad day, she would ask them to complete a classroom task or to help her with something like carrying her keys or clipboard in the hall or being in charge of reminding her to grab her lunch bag before everyone headed to lunch. If you asked any of her students, they would all remember the times they got to be her assistant. The love and extra attention were spread over the whole class day after day. Her gift was relating to the students and knowing when they needed the boost.

"She also had the patience to break the cycle of disruption and negative attention that many students find themselves in, by giving them quiet, nonchalant ways to have her attention. Kelly taught me how to give those challenging kids recognition and care—and the value of doing so. Kelly worked every day to give a little extra love when students needed it the most.

"Of course, sometimes this is more easily said than done, and it doesn't apply to extreme situations. If two students get into a physical altercation in your classroom, you aren't going to make things better by giving them a classroom task five minutes later. But the next day those students may be feeling a little embarrassed or exposed. This is the time to greet them with a warm smile and distract them with a task to remind them that they are a welcome and essential part of the class. I've never regretted giving any of my students attention and love."

Strategy 12: Anchor Your Classroom with Mirrors, Windows, and Sliding Glass Doors

You may be familiar with the concept of literature serving as mirrors, windows, and sliding glass doors. Several decades ago, Emily Style ([1988] 1996) shared the idea that students should be exposed to literature and other educational materials that both reflect their own identities and experiences (mirrors) and introduce them to new perspectives and experiences (windows). Later, Rudine Sims Bishop (1990) extended the metaphor to include not only mirrors and windows but also tools to navigate them (sliding glass doors).

Mirrors allow students to see themselves reflected in the curriculum, which can help them build a positive sense of their identity. Mirrors show students that they matter, that their stories and cultures are significant enough to hold space in the classroom. When students do not see themselves represented in the curriculum, they are at risk of internalizing a sense of unimportance. Teachers who deliberately ensure mirrors in the classroom—books, activities, and visuals that represent children's and families' races, cultures, identities, and interests—are emphatically telling students that they matter.

Windows allow students to see beyond their own experiences and gain a deeper understanding of the world around them. This can help build empathy and understanding toward others and foster a more inclusive and compassionate community. This means that students need to be exposed to the full spectrum of human diversity throughout the school day. A wide range of races, cultures, identities, and interests inclusive of and beyond the identities of your students should be represented in literature, textbooks, and physical imagery in the classroom.

Sliding doors represent the opportunities students need to explore and navigate different perspectives and experiences of others. By giving students tools to explore beyond their own experiences and backgrounds, we can help them grow and learn in the present and prepare them for the diverse and complex world they will encounter in the future. Activities that support this might include creating pen pals with students from

Chapter 3: Love and Care in Teaching

other cultures, deliberately partnering students with different identities, and engaging students in project-based learning with members of the wider community.

To create mirrors, windows, and sliding doors in the classroom, make learning about your students' individual identities your starting place.

STUDENT SPOTLIGHT

Caring Teachers

"You can tell when a teacher cares about you when they express interest in not just school-related things, but also in your life outside of school. One of my teachers takes time out of the beginning of each class to go around in a circle and ask how everyone's week, weekend, or day has been. If a student just replies with "good," he says that's not an acceptable answer. He wants to actually know something we did and how we choose to spend our time so he can learn more about us. I can really tell that he cares because he usually remembers what you tell him. He will bring it up in a future conversation, which shows that he was listening and actually takes an interest in your life."—*high school student*

• • •

"In third grade, our teacher gave us a snack at 2:00 every day. She never had to do this but she felt it was right. It made me feel good that our teacher cared enough about us to give us a little break at the end of the day. This was also important for me because as a younger kid I tend to get bored easily and the break meant a lot to me personally."—*elementary school student*

• • •

"I switched schools in the middle of the year and my math teacher took me under her wing. By the end of the first week, I knew I had someone who cared about me."—*elementary school student*

• • •

"I can tell a teacher feels caring towards students when students feel safe in a classroom environment. I can tell when a teacher cares about their students through their tone and how they talk to the students in the classroom. One of my teachers demonstrated that they were caring toward me when I came to them about an issue with another teacher. They gave me a very good view on the other teacher's perspective, but also I could recognize that they cared for me because they were empathizing with me."—*middle school student*

• • •

"You can tell that a teacher cares about you in the little things, like if they make an effort to talk to you or if they notice things about your life."—*high school student*

• • •

"You can tell when a teacher cares about you when they listen to you and they call on you and they don't just let you sit over there—they actually pick you for something." —*elementary school student*

• • •

"It is important for teachers to care about you because if they don't care about the students, they will not teach us as well. You need a good relationship with your teacher to learn as much as you can. When teachers care about you as person, they care about how well you do at school."—*elementary school student*

Strategy 13: Help Students Express and Share Their Identities

Teachers and education scholars know that classrooms are becoming increasingly diverse. It's important to keep in mind that classrooms always contained students with diverse backgrounds and identities. Identity includes the visible and invisible characteristics of a person such as ethnicity, race, culture, gender, sexual orientation, geographic origin, affinities, interests, group memberships, and so on. Even if your school appears homogenous—perhaps it serves an all-Asian or all-white community, or you teach at a religious school where students all identify as Muslim or Christian or Jewish—there are many differences among your students.

According to Gholdy Muhammad (2020), identity consists of who others say we are, who we think we are, and who we hope to become. There are many ways you can explore and affirm your students' identities. Muhammad makes the case that students should be invited to share who they are and how they identify and should see themselves reflected in the physical space of the classroom and in the curriculum. Following her advice, this chapter includes identity-affirming instructional activities as well as strategies for providing affirming spaces and classroom resources.

"This Is Me" People Posters

This activity offers an engaging way for students of any grade level to consider and convey key aspects of their personal identity. To help students understand and express their identity, begin with self-reflection.

Chapter 3: Love and Care in Teaching

73

With younger students, you might start with a brief example and discussion. For example:

"Have you ever thought about what makes you *you*? I can think of some things that make me *me*. One thing is that my parents came to this country from Bosnia. In my family, we speak both English and Bosnian. Another thing is that I am a dad to two children who I love very much. I am your teacher, and it makes me happy to be with you each day because I love helping you learn new things. I like to read books and go for walks with my dog, Max, because quiet time helps me relax."

Then invite students to share their own examples of what makes them *them*. They might talk in pairs or small groups to reflect and generate their ideas, then share with the class. Be sure to coach your students to explain *why* they like certain activities. You want to move beyond likes and dislikes to deeper-level insights. You might say, "Notice how I shared why I like teaching, reading books, and going for walks. What new things can you learn about me when I tell you *why* I like those things?" Responses might include "You like helping others" and "You need quiet times to relax." Then ask, "What can we learn about *you* when you tell us things you like to do?" With the insights you gain, you can start to think through which students might need quiet breaks throughout the day, which students would be the best fit for classroom jobs or peer tutoring, and more.

With older students, ask them more explicitly to take a few minutes to reflect on their identity. On their own or in small groups, ask them to describe important parts of themselves, such as:

- race
- ethnicity
- family's country of origin
- current geographic location
- languages they speak
- religion
- gender
- other visible physical features
- passions and interests
- favorite activities
- hobbies
- other invisible or internal features

Then provide students with sheets of butcher paper or other paper large enough to fit a student's entire body and ask them to have a friend outline their body. Then invite them to use the ideas they've discussed or thought about to create a visual representation of important parts of their identity (of what makes them *them*). Students can draw or write on the body image, cut pictures from a magazine, or print images to include. Alternatively, have students fill in the "This Is Me" template (page 88).

Gallery Walk

Once the images are complete, hang them in the classroom or hallway. Then conduct a gallery walk. Give each student sticky notes and have them silently walk around to view the identity artwork, placing sticky notes on each piece of art to share the ways they are different from or similar to their classmates. For younger students you may want to provide writing prompts, such as:

- Your family is from . . . Mine is from . . .
- Your father speaks . . . My father speaks . . .
- You really like . . . I really like . . .
- We are both . . .

Once the gallery walk is over, have students return to their own artwork to read the sticky notes. Then gather students in a circle to discuss and reflect together, using questions like these:

- After your gallery walk, what did you notice and what did you wonder?
- How did it feel to share your identity (what makes you *you*) with your classmates?
- What similarities and differences did you notice?
- What surprised you, if anything, and why?
- What will you think about most after completing this activity and why?
- Why do you think we did the activity?
- What will you tell your family about this activity?
- Complete this sentence: "I used to think . . . and now I think . . ."

As an extension of this activity, you may decide to make a classroom figure that incorporates everyone's identities into one piece of art, such as a wall-sized silhouette with each student's individual personal depiction inside.

Figure 3.1 This Is Me

The student in this example speaks Spanish, identifies as Jewish with English heritage, has a cat, and loves to read comics and ride a scooter.

Chapter 3: Love and Care in Teaching

Strategy 14: Help Students Consider How They See Themselves and How Others See Them

Identity includes how we see ourselves and how others see us. In your classroom, you can encourage students to consider how they see themselves and others as individuals and in their roles with the people in their lives.

There are two main learning goals related to this process. First, you can help your students think through the ways in which they allow other's views to influence the way they think about themselves. In some instances, this influence can be identity affirming. For example, a student may share, "My family describes me as kind and sporty. This makes me feel good because I do try to be kind and I love playing sports." In other instances, this influence can negate identity. For example, a student may share, "I am short for my age and lots of people talk to me like a baby. But I'm not a baby, I'm much older!" Besides guiding your students to think about the differences between the ways someone might view them and the ways they view themselves, you can also help them distinguish between which outsider views might be helpful and which they want to reject.

Second, understanding that how we see ourselves can be different from how others might see us is key to building empathy and curiosity about others. For instance, a student might share, "I wear my hair long, and a lot of times older folks who don't know me talk to me like I'm a girl, even though I'm a boy." Once your students understand potential mismatches between how they view themselves and how others view them, you can help them think more critically about how they can work against making assumptions about others.

To introduce this activity, you might say, "Today we are going to talk about who we are and who others think we are. We will share what it feels like when someone cares about how you see yourself—your *identity*—and what it feels like when someone might describe you in a way that is *not* true. Then we'll talk about how to show your class-mates that you care about their identity and why it might hurt someone's feelings if we make wrong guesses, or *assumptions*, about someone's identity."

Setting the Stage

To help students understand the concept of identity, you might decide to do a word splash. Write *identity* in the middle of the board. Using the children's ideas from the "This Is Me" activity, guide students to generate different types of social identities and words that describe people. As students share, add the words and images to the board.

Next, ask, "What does it mean if someone describes you in a positive way? How does it feel?" Probe for examples related to school. After a few ideas are shared, point out that when we feel like people like and understand us, we feel a sense of belonging and connection.

Then, ask, "What does it mean if people describe you in a way that is not true? How does it feel?" Again, encourage school-related examples and help students recognize that this can lead to feeling misunderstood and disconnected.

After discussing differences among classmates, say: "Think about friends you spend time with. Are they just like you? How do you know how your friends see themselves? What are ways that you're alike? How are you different from each other? Does it matter that you and your friends are different? Why or why not?" Help students make connections to the idea that differences are to be celebrated and honored and do not limit friendships.

Finally, summarize: "Our identity is important because it is who we are—and who we are matters. We want to feel like we belong. It feels good when people care about who we are. It can feel bad when people are wrong about who they think we are or don't care about who we are."

Once students understand what identity is and the connections between identity, caring, and sense of belonging, select one of the following two options based on the grade level and skills of your students.

Partner Sharing

This activity works well with younger students, though students of all ages might enjoy it. Place your students in pairs; in each pair, one student is Partner 1 and one is Partner 2. Say:

> "Partner 1, tell your partner one true thing about who you are." (Give examples as needed: *I'm a girl; I play soccer; I'm Black; I'm an artist; I'm Jewish; I collect shells.*) "Then tell your partner what you like about this part of your identity." (*I love when I kick the ball far; I love singing at synagogue; It's fun to look for shells by the ocean.*)

> "Partner 2, put both hands on your head if you already knew what your partner shared with you. Or, if you were surprised and learned something new about your partner, put both hands in the air. Keep your hands where they are. Wow, look around. What do you notice?"

Pause to debrief. Discuss what was surprising and why and what was already known and why. You might point out that even though you think you can see parts of someone's identity, it does not always mean that is how the person sees themself. And you might point out that some parts of identity are invisible or can't be known at all by looking at someone.

Before continuing the activity, say: "Learning more about each other can be surprising. The surprises teach us that we should not think that we already know all about someone's identity or what makes them *them*. When people think they know

Chapter 3: Love and Care in Teaching

77

something that they don't, it is called an *assumption*." (Write the word on the board.) "An assumption is like a guess that is very often a mistake. All of us, adults too, make assumptions, or mistakes, about people. These mistakes cause misunderstandings and hurt feelings. In our classroom, we want to stay curious about each other and try hard not to make mistakes, or assumptions, that could hurt someone's feelings or cause misunderstandings."

Be prepared to give an example or two of assumptions, or ask students to share an example of a time this happened to them. Then have partners switch roles and share again. Repeat this process for two or three rotations, or for however long time allows and students remain engaged. Be sure to pause and debrief each time. At the close of the activity, ask:

- How might you learn more about your classmates' identities?
- How might you share more about your identity with your classmates?
- What can you do if someone describes a mistaken assumption about you?
- What can you do so that you do not describe someone in a way that could be a mistaken assumption?

Who Is the Me That Others See?

If you work with older elementary or middle school students, share the "Who Is the Me That Others See?" form (page 89). Introduce and explain the form, using questions like these to prompt students' reflection:

- "Think about the places in your life. Where are you most yourself? Where do you feel the freest to be yourself?" (place of worship, barbershop, friend's home, family living room) "Who are the people in these places? How would these people describe you?" (male, Hispanic, athlete, funny, outgoing, kind)

- "Who are the people that are most important to you and why? Think about all the people in your life, not just the people you live with or your best friends but also favorite teachers, neighbors, and other people who know you well. How would these people describe you?"

- "Who are the people in your family? How would your family describe you?"

- "One part of your identity is 'student.' Which parts of your identity are important for your classmates to know? Why? Which parts of your identity are important for your teachers to know? Why? In what ways can (or have) your teachers and classmates show (or shown) that they care (or cared) about these parts of your identity?"

Next, ask students to complete the "Who Is the Me That Others See?" form. Allow time for this in class if possible. This will encourage students to stay engaged in understanding and affirming their identity.

As closure, invite some students to share ideas they've written and guide the class to affirm this sharing. Students should not feel obligated to share what they've written. You might also consider one (or both) of the following closure activities.

Group sharing

Using a shared online tool such as a Google Doc, create a two-columned document so students can post their responses to the following prompt: "You have just reflected on how others see you and the way their views affect how you think about yourself. What advice would you give to a fellow classmate if someone viewed them in a way that was untrue, unfair, or hurtful? What advice would you give teachers about how to make sure that students' identities matter in the classroom?"

Speed summary reflection

Gather students in a circle and say, "Think of one word, or very short phrase, that describes how it feels when someone you care about sees (or affirms) your identity. Don't say your words aloud yet." After at least two minutes of wait time, have students share out loud—one by one in rapid succession with no discussion. Repeat the process, asking, "Think of one word, or very short phrase, that describes how it feels when someone does not care about your identity or gets your identity wrong." Wait two minutes and share again in rapid succession.

Then, ask, "What did you notice after listening to everyone's answers? What did you wonder about?" You might offer an example, such as, "I noticed many powerful positive feelings about when identity is affirmed, and many painful negative feelings about when identity *isn't* affirmed. I am wondering more about what I can do to make sure that I am affirming the identity of each of you in our classroom and in our school."

Strategy 15: Make All Classroom Spaces Affirming Places

As a teacher, you have a lot of control about what your classroom looks like, including the physical layout of furniture, classroom displays, artwork, lighting, and more. In this activity, you will think through and plan ways to create an identity-affirming classroom space.

Charting Information About Students' Identities

Start by making a chart that notes key aspects of your students' identities. Use knowledge from this chapter and from information you've compiled about students' funds of knowledge, family expectations, and goals (chapter 1); from any family visits your class has had a chance to experience (chapter 2); and from other information you've discovered through interactions with your students. For example, you could use the "This Is Me" activity or the "All About Me" questionnaire (chapter 1) to record all the

Chapter 3: Love and Care in Teaching   **79**

different aspects of students' self-reported identities. Figure 3.2 offers an example (see the blank form on page 91). You will notice a column for "additional attributes." Here you will make note of any student information that will contribute to your ability to plan a classroom space that affirms students and addresses their needs.

Classroom Spaces Inventory

Also take inventory of your classroom spaces. Create a matrix like the example in figure 3.3 (see the blank form on page 92) to record an inventory of different spaces represented in your classroom and the ways these spaces and materials affirm (or do not affirm) your students' identities. Consider questions like these:

- Who is depicted in classroom posters?
- Which identities are written about in the books of my classroom library?
- In what ways do students have opportunities to contribute to classroom artwork and other physical features of the room?
- Am I providing adequate access to mirrors and windows?

Figure 3.2 Student Identity Data Chart

Race	Gender	Religion	Cultural Aspects (food, clothing, traditions, holidays)	Languages	Affinities/ Interests	Additional Attributes
White Black Latino Asian	Cis—male Cis—female Trans—male	Muslim Jewish Christian Non-affiliated	Christmas Saris Lunar New Year	Spanish Mandarin English ASL	Biking Football Soccer Drama Reading Movies Gaming	Wheelchair Light sensitivity Hearing impaired

Figure 3.3 Classroom Spaces Inventory

	Classroom Posters	Classroom Library	Students' Visual Contributions
Identities Represented	English language Black, white races Cisgender	English language Black, white authors Black, white characters Cisgender characters/authors Dual-parent families	English language
Identities Missing	Asian Latino LGBTQIA+	Multilingual Asian and Latino authors/characters LGBTQIA+ authors/ characters	No imagery provided by students at all

Planning for an Affirming and Inclusive Classroom

After this inventory, you may notice that all classroom posters are written solely in English while your classroom includes many children with multilingual backgrounds. Or you may realize that few of the books in your classroom library depict diverse family structures while you have students in your classroom who have two fathers or who live with their grandparents. Come up with ways to reflect the identities of all your students and their families more fully. Ask yourself:

- What will I do to make my classroom space more inclusive and representative of my students' identities?
- How will I include materials that serve as windows and mirrors?
- What barriers do I have? Who can help me navigate the barriers?
- What resources do I need? What additional information do I need to access? Who can help me with my plan?
- What role can students play in creating or identifying materials for our classroom?

Strategy 16: Connect with Journaling and Letter Writing

Most teachers want their students to know that they care for them and want to find ways to build a relationship of trust with their students. Inviting students to write to you through journaling or letters can be very helpful for this purpose.

Two-Way Journals

Two-way journal exchanges with students can help you build trust and express care, because you're giving your students an opportunity to share and you're actively listening and providing individualized responses. Daily or weekly, depending on your own time constraints, you can provide a journal-writing prompt. In the journal, a student responds to the prompt, and you write a reply or comment back.

If this process is too arduous, consider using two-way journals with only those students with whom other methods you've tried for relationship and trust building have been ineffective. Figure 3.4 offers examples of prompts and shows how each prompt can be useful in expressing love and care and building rapport.

What about when students share sensitive issues? You are not a counselor or therapist. Your role is to respond in ways that validate your students' experiences, help them identify feelings, express empathy, support their problem-solving skills, and connect them to resources. The University of California–Berkeley's Greater Good Science Center has an online source for educators. At the Greater Good in Education website, you can find practices for using dialogue journals with elementary, middle, and

Chapter 3: Love and Care in Teaching   **81**

high school students. These offer a range of examples of empathic teacher responses from professor and school psychology expert Dr. Mary Lynn Crow. Go to ggie.berkeley.edu and type "dialogue journals" in the search box.

Figure 3.4 Prompts for Two-Way Journaling

Prompts	Rationale
"Tell me something that happened today that made you feel successful or good about yourself."	It's easy for busy teachers to miss opportunities to affirm students' successes. Other times teachers may not even notice when a student experiences personal success. This prompt provides an opportunity for teachers to offer affirming and congratulatory remarks for a student who has accomplished something that is personally meaningful.
"If you could change one thing about the school day, what would it be and why?"	Teachers who use this prompt could make realistic adjustments to students' days based on responses to this prompt. In addition to writing a response to the student, an actionable step that addresses the student's desire goes a long way to building trust. Even if the adjustment is not possible, an affirming response that validates the student is helpful in expressing care.
"If you had three wishes, what would you wish for and why?"	This whimsical prompt might yield fantastical responses (*I wish I had a million dollars*). It can also lead to deep trust building between students and teachers. The prompt might unearth social issues in school (*I wish my friends would let me play with them at recess*) or challenges at home (*I wish my parents would stop fighting*). Whatever the responses, this prompt helps the teacher learn more about students' inner desires and build bonds of understanding.
"Write about a time when you wish you had spoken up or done something differently. What happened? If you could do it again, what would you do differently?"	This prompt, geared towards older students, can lead to lesson plans for the entire class. For example, if some students report feeling unhappy about playing the role of bystander while a classmate was being bullied, the teacher can invite all students to create role-playing scenarios for use during class time. Students might also share that they wish they had studied more for an exam, tried out for a role in the school play, or been more truthful with their parents. Each of these topics allows for a meaningful response from the teacher. Commiserating, sharing a similar experience, or simply validating the students' feelings all help students feel connected and cared for in their classroom.

Anonymous Mailbox

Some students may be hesitant to share private information in their two-way journals, since although the information is confidential, it isn't anonymous. Students may have unfavorable views of decisions or assignments you've made but not feel comfortable sharing these thoughts directly or they may have questions they're embarrassed to ask. A mailbox designated for questions and comments, with the option to remain anonymous, lets students safely share their thoughts, feelings, and worries and provides you with information and insights you might otherwise not learn.

Think carefully about where you will place the mailbox and the procedures you want students to follow when using it. In some classrooms it makes sense to set an honor system, using a decorated shoebox with a slit in the lid. Or you may wish to secure the box with a simple lock. You can also purchase an inexpensive locking box, such as a money box, online. Consider placing the mailbox in a space where students frequently spend time (such as a reading corner or technology area), or place the box by your classroom door, allowing students to leave notes on their way in or out of the room. Some teachers ask that all students put something in the box at least once a week, whether it's a note, a drawing, or a blank sheet of paper. This approach eliminates the potential stigma someone might feel when others see them leaving you a note.

When you introduce the mailbox, be sure to explain why the mailbox is useful to you and to students. For example, you could say, "This box is going to be our Questions and Comments Mailbox. The mailbox lets you bring something to my attention without feeling self-conscious or embarrassed, or worried about getting in trouble. And the mailbox is useful to me because what you write will help me know about your ideas, concerns, and questions so I can respond to them. Sometimes you might even be brave enough to write about an issue that is important to everyone in the classroom."

Share some examples of appropriate things students might decide to put into the mailbox and how you might respond. For example:

- "Someone might put in a note that says they need extra math help before the next test but are embarrassed to ask for it. That would make me think about how I can offer math tutoring after school, or plan an extra-help math session for small-group time, or write websites on the board that students could use to brush up on the math concepts that will be on the test. Not only could these ideas help the person who wrote the note—they could also mean extra math help for other students."

- "If I received a note from a student who wanted to sit in a different seat, I could switch a few students' seating assignments or I could set up groups that give students more opportunities to switch seats."

- "If someone confided in me that a student was being left out on the playground, I could read a book to the class about how to make everyone feel included on the playground. Or we could talk as a class about fun things to do on the playground and practice how to ask our classmates to join in."

After you explain the purpose of the mailbox, share your expectations for how students will use it. Be sure to let students know that they may include their name if they wish to, though they are not required to sign the notes they put in the box. Explain that including their name is especially important if they have a serious concern, big worry, or need urgent help. Reinforce that students are welcome to come speak to you at any time and that you are always available for support. The mailbox should not be positioned as a substitute for a face-to-face request for help.

> ## SENSITIVE OR DISTURBING TOPICS
>
> When you're unsure how to respond to a journal entry, mailbox comment, or any sensitive concern raised by a student, reach out to a school counselor or psychologist for guidance. And if students raise issues about abuse, harm, suicide, guns, or other serious issues that put children at risk, it's essential to follow your school's policies for mandatory reporting.

Chapter 3: Love and Care in Teaching

The essential part of this tool is that you address the comments and questions in the mailbox. Read the contents of the box privately. You might find a note about a classroom interaction that hurt a student's feelings or a suggestion for improving some aspect of the school day. As appropriate, plan to share ideas and issues raised with the whole class, perhaps once a week. Prepare what you will say ahead of time so you have thought through ways to address the issues and how to talk about them with the class. Some student notes may require additional work on your part to research solutions or reach out to colleagues or other school personnel.

Strategy 17: Set Norms Together to Build a Classroom Community

A strong classroom community is one where students and teachers feel emotional safety and delight in each other's successes while providing empathy and support during challenging times. Building a classroom community takes time and deliberate effort. Elevating student voice and sharing some classroom decision-making with students are central approaches to supporting an environment where students feel loved and cared for by their teacher and respected and supported by each other.

Collaborating to create norms is a key to developing this community and is important in classrooms at all grade levels. It can be a powerful way to build emotional and intellectual safety and guide your classroom interactions in caring and loving ways.

Brainstorming Norms

Start with a group discussion. How you go about this will depend on the ages of your students.

When working with younger students, explain that norms are like rules, but everyone in the classroom gets to decide on them. You might help children understand by describing norms as expectations. Ask students: "What are you expected to do when you go to a movie theater? After eating a picnic in a park?"

As students share, write their ideas on the board. Point out how the place connects with the expectations or norms: movie theater—whisper or don't talk; picnic—throw your trash and recyclables in the bins or take them away with you.

Then say: "Today we're going to talk together to agree on some norms that make sense for us to follow in the classroom." Explain that the purpose of setting classroom norms is to make sure it's a place where everyone feels safe and welcome, where everyone belongs. When students feel like they belong, they will feel good about being in the classroom. That good feeling can help them get along with each other, do better in school, and have more fun.

84

When You're the New Teacher

Figure 3.5 Sample Norms Word Cloud

Place students in small groups of three or four students, and ask each group to think about one or two norms that would help everyone feel safe and welcome in the classroom.

When working with older students, explain that you want them to work together to establish classroom norms. Discuss the meaning of norms—group goals or agreements for how people in the class will behave so that everyone in the classroom experiences a sense of belonging and mutual respect. Then ask students to complete the "Norms Questionnaire" (page 93).

Once students have completed the questionnaire, arrange them in small groups of four to six students. Ask them to first share their responses to the prompts and then work together to come up with two or three classroom norms that would lead to the type of classroom community they described and shared.

Choosing and Displaying Norms

Next, bring the whole class back together and invite each group to share their norms aloud. As groups share, write the norms on the board. If duplicate or similar norms are shared, use a check mark next to the norm to indicate repetitive ideas. Once all norms are shared and recorded, ask students to explain how these norms, if followed, would create a welcoming classroom community where everyone belongs.

You may have in mind a norm that is missing; if so, describe it and explain why you would like it included.

Consider using a word cloud to help students create norms. Using a Google Doc or other shared document, ask students to write words that describe their ideal classroom.

When they've finished, copy everyone's words into an online word cloud generator to create a word cloud. The generator uses font size and type density to visually represent the frequency of the ideas students shared. Students then view the word cloud and decide on norms that everyone should follow, making sure to address the ideas that are biggest and boldest. Figure 3.5 shows an example of a word cloud from a norms-setting activity.

Finally, create a classroom visual that displays the norms, such as the example in figure 3.6. If you've made a word cloud, the size of the words can help you and your students focus on five or six norms that are most important in your classroom. Post the classroom norms where they're easily seen, and refer to them regularly to remind students of norms. It is a good idea to continue to revisit the norms to provide a chance to discuss how they are supporting the class and to monitor problems in using them. You may want to make and print copies of the norms for students to sign or to send home to parents.

Figure 3.6 Sample Seventh Grade Classroom Norms

- Your voice is important. Raise your hand to be heard.
- Your participation helps everyone. Be prepared and remain engaged.
- We all want to grow. Share your thinking and seek feedback.
- We can learn from each other. Listen and ask respectful questions.
- We all matter. Be caring and kind to all members of our classroom community.

Strategy 18: Have a Shout-Out Box for Student Affirmations

Students' and teachers' interest in each other is the foundation for creating a caring and loving environment. The shout-out box is a great companion activity to any of the many social emotional learning models adopted by districts or schools, one that offers students a way to express love, care, and appreciation for each other.

The directions for the shout-out box are simple. First, explain the purpose of the box. You might say, "I want to share a fun way you can show that you care about your classmates. We're going to start using a shout-out box. Who knows what a shout-out is? That's right, a shout-out is when you call someone out for doing something awesome. Every week, I will read the shouts-outs aloud and you can hear the great things you say about each other. Does anyone have ideas about comments that someone could put in the shout-out box?" Offer examples as needed, such as the following:

- "Malik invited me to play kickball and even let me pick my own position. It made me feel really good. That was so awesome!"
- "I had trouble with the math work today and Terri helped me out. What a relief!"
- "Adrianne, Sandra, and Marcie were all sitting together at lunch, and they noticed me sitting by myself. Sandra invited me to eat with them. That was kind."

The pattern and format you are teaching with these samples is the use of an explicit scenario or example and then a statement about the person. Invite students to contribute to the box at any time. If the same students often receive shout-outs while other students rarely or never receive any mentions, you may decide to encourage students to write a shout-out to a different person each time. Or you might consider assigning weekly shout-out partners where each partner provides a shout-out for the other at least once during that week. You can write your own shout-outs as well, since the writer remains anonymous.

You will determine when and how often you read the shout-outs. In my classroom, I decided to close each day by reading them aloud just before dismissal. It was a delightful way to punctuate the school day with love and positivity!

• • •

This chapter helped you understand the role of love and care in the classroom. You now have concrete strategies and actions to engage in the following:

- expressing love and care for your students
- creating identify-affirming lessons and spaces
- building a classroom community where students have a sense of belonging and care for one another

Name: _____ Date: _____

This Is Me

Directions: Inside the shape, write words and draw pictures that tell things about you and things that are important to you.

Name: _____

Date: _____

Who Is the Me That Others See?

Directions: First, reflect on how others see you. Write notes about your ideas in the chart.

Person, people, group	What social identities do they think describe me? (such as race, gender, religion, language, ability, age, and so on)	What words or phrases would they use to describe my identity? (characteristics, traits, talents, interests)	Does this match how I see myself? In what ways?	Is this different from how I see myself? In what ways?

(continued →)

When You're the New Teacher: 28 Strategies to Align Your Good Intentions with Your Teaching Practices

© Elizabeth Soslau—Free Spirit Publishing

(*continued*)

Directions: Next, think about these questions. Write your answers on a sheet of paper.

1. Is it important to you that other people view you the way you view yourself? Why or why not?

2. How does your relationship with someone relate to whether you feel their views about you are important? Why?

3. What can you learn about yourself through other people's eyes?

4. What might you reject about how others see you? What might you accept? Why?

5. What do you wish other people knew about you, but don't?

6. What are ways you can show who you are so others can know you better?

7. What do you wish others would ask you so that you could share more about who you are?

8. What can teachers do to make it possible for you to share who you are in the classroom?

Student Identity Data

Race	Gender	Religion	Cultural Aspects (food, culture, traditions, holidays)	Languages	Affinities/ Interests	Other

When You're the New Teacher: 28 Strategies to Align Your Good Intentions with Your Teaching Practices

© Elizabeth Soslau—Free Spirit Publishing

Classroom Spaces Inventory

	Classroom Posters	Classroom Library	Students' Visual Contributions
Identities Represented			
Identities Missing			

When You're the New Teacher: 28 Strategies to Align Your Good Intentions with Your Teaching Practices

Full name: _____ **Date:** _____

I prefer to be called: _____

My pronouns are: _____

Norms Questionnaire

Directions: Write your answers to the questions. You will share your answers with your classmates.

1. My expectations of my teacher are:

2. My expectations of my classmates are:

3. When I am in this class, I want to feel:

4. When I think about sharing my opinions and thoughts in class, I hope:

5. Words that describe an ideal classroom environment are:

4

Embracing Opportunities for Growth

Strategies for Navigating Challenges, Building Expertise, and Sustaining Joy

Teaching is not without challenges. There will always be obstacles to navigate and hard moments to work through. As issues arise, you will have opportunities to develop your collaborative expertise. Development of collaborative skills will contribute to your success throughout the early years of teaching and will serve you well as your career progresses.

This chapter addresses four main challenges that are likely to arise throughout your tenure as a teacher. Through reflection and practice, you will explore and answer the following questions:

- How can I respond when someone I work with says or does something I know isn't right or fair for students?
- Where, when, and how can I seek help with challenges and problems I face in my work?
- What are effective ways I can overcome personal barriers and share my own expertise with colleagues?
- How can I deal with professional stress, maintain emotional well-being, and bring joy to my teaching?

Collaborative expertise is the set of skills that enables you to speak up, seek help, and contribute ideas. It is one thing to know that something needs to be done, and a very different thing to do it. To develop and enact these skills, you need practice. This chapter provides direction for you to plan and rehearse ways to hone your collaborative expertise. Through reflective writing and activities, you can practice applying these skills to real-life scenarios.

Strategy 19: Follow a Recipe for Addressing Problematic Situations with Colleagues

What do you do when you witness problematic teacher decision-making that adversely impacts students, the classroom culture, or the school community? Every teacher has experienced a gut-check moment—an instance when they know that another person's words, choices, or actions will cause harm.

TEACHER SPOTLIGHT

I Wish I Had . . .

"I had a student who liked to eat lunch in my room, but her teacher (whose class she was assigned to at lunchtime) told me she wasn't allowed to until her behavior improved in his class. A few days later, I jokingly asked the teacher if the student was still 'grounded,' because she kept asking to have lunch with me. He laughed and said he doubted she could even spell *grounded*. I didn't expect to hear a teacher talk like that about a student, and it made me uncomfortable. As a not-so-great student in middle school myself, I could imagine my own teachers thinking or saying similar things about me. I wish I had stood up for this student, but it was my first year and I was afraid to make too many waves with the other teachers."

Many teachers feel ill-equipped to speak up and address harmful schooling perspectives and practices. Common responses like "I didn't know what to say," "I was shocked," or "I was caught off guard" do nothing to help. What *can* help is engaging in the challenging but important process of collaborative problem solving to address harm.

Inspired by my attendance at a racial literacy workshop created and led by Dr. Howard Stevenson, I offer a version of his approach to problematic moments. You will practice using this framework, based largely on Stevenson's work, to engage your colleagues in conversations that move toward more culturally responsive and sustaining decision-making.

As both an educator and a psychologist, Stevenson developed an approach to support people involved in a racially contentious and stressful encounter. The emphasis in his approach is on healthy responses—ways people can resolve a racially stressful moment while protecting their own emotional well-being. In the following pages, I lay out an adapted version of his approach, using Stevenson's same vocabulary with slightly different definitions and applications. While his framework is intended to address racially stressful encounters, I apply his work to any stressful encounter with people who express derogatory views and beliefs.

It is also important to note that this framework is about you, the person who speaks up. While this approach has the potential to help your colleagues think differently or reconsider their beliefs and actions, people must have the will to make a change. All you can do is plant the seed. Shifting their thinking is not your responsibility; naming what you know to be right is. The purpose of the framework is to ensure that you walk away from these stressful interactions feeling whole, knowing that you both spoke up and out against unfair, disparaging, or biased beliefs and actions and took care of yourself by doing so. Stevenson's work shows that if you silently swallow and ignore the inner turmoil that results from engaging in these unhealthy encounters, you are psychologically and physically harming yourself (Stevenson 2014). Further, you miss the opportunity to disrupt practices that would cause students to feel distress. No teacher wants to be a silent bystander when children are being harmed.

I like to think of Stevenson's ideas as a series of ingredients*:

- affection—affirming the person, their goals, their identity, and their feelings
- correction—providing new facts, posing an alternative view, or referring to a resource
- protection—monitoring how the response (correction) is being received
- connection—linking the new framing (correction) to the person's original goals and future improved interactions

The four-part recipe can be adapted to the needs of the situation and the people involved. The ingredients do not need to be used in a specific sequence, and using equal measures of the ingredients is less important than being sure to include each of them.

Putting the Ingredients Together: An Example

Imagine you are in the teachers' lounge having a working lunch with teachers in your grade group. The teachers are discussing a grammar lesson where they will post tweets from celebrities on the board and have their students correct the tweet authors' grammar. As you and the grade team pour over the examples of tweets to be used, you realize that most of the tweeters are African American. Collectively, the tweets make up rich examples of African American Vernacular English (AAVE) and *are* grammatically correct, but the other teachers are labeling them as incorrect. You know from your own experience or from learning about AAVE in your teacher preparation program that AAVE is a valid way of communicating and expressing ideas. You know that the planned

---

*Used with permission of Howard C. Stevenson. Stevenson has since re-sequenced the elements for his approach to protection, affection, correction, and connection transactions, or PACCT, which undergirds racial literacy workshops provided by Lion's Story (lionsstory.org).

lesson will send a harmful and inaccurate message about valid ways of communicating to the students.

What do you do? You know that speaking up and stating why the planned approach is harmful, and what approach you suggest instead, is critical to your students' well-being. Ideally, you want your participation in this discussion to be perceived as collegial and make way for productive collaboration. There are many possible ways you can speak up and speak out during this conversation. Below is one such way, using the four ingredients for navigating challenging conversations mentioned above.

You: I want to make sure I understand your ideas for the lesson. It sounds like you want students to correct tweets that you've identified as examples of incorrect grammar. Is that right?

Teacher 1: Yes. The kids will love it. They love social media and many of the tweet authors will be familiar to them. It's a good way to make sure our instruction is relevant.

Teacher 2: Grammar can be dry and boring. This will make it fun.

You: Okay, I see. I know you want to create an engaging grammar lesson that kids can relate to. That's what great teaching is all about [*affection*]. I think the directions need to be different, though. Asking students to correct the grammar is problematic because the grammar in the tweets is a recognized way to communicate [*correction*]. It's called AAVE—African American Vernacular English. It has strong historical roots and cultural connections [*correction*]. I think we could lead the students in a conversation about AAVE. We could explicitly recognize and validate grammar patterns in ways that people communicate [*correction*]. Then, instead of having students correct the tweets, we could ask them to rewrite the tweets for different audiences and situations [*correction*].

I know we're all committed to looking closely at the messages we send to students and making sure we're not disparaging people or communities [*connection*]. So does that make sense? What do you think? Does anyone have other ideas [*protection*]?

This teacher's response to the lesson planning may sound magical and too good to be true. It is not. This is a true reflection of what I have witnessed in my own practice. When you know the ingredients and you diligently practice, you too can speak up and speak out.

Your Turn to Practice: Another Example

Here's a vignette you can use as a starting point to practice using the four ingredients. Imagine yourself in this scenario with a classroom teacher.

Classroom teacher: We need to plan for literacy lessons. Next week we'll begin a unit on poetry. I thought it would be fun to have the students analyze Amanda Gorman's inauguration poem, "The Hill We Climb." She was the first-ever National Youth Poet Laureate and I think our kids would love reading work from a young person.

You: I love that idea! I'll do some research about Amanda Gorman. I know she's a poet and a political activist who writes about all kinds of exciting issues. But I need to learn more about her and the historical and political context that she responds to in her poetry.

Classroom teacher: I'm so excited that you're willing to learn more and do the research to get prepared for the unit. I need you to know we won't be addressing any political tensions or discussing her role as an activist. The beginning of our poetry unit is focused on form and structure. We won't get into symbolism, metaphors, and similes until later in the unit. And, of course, we will use less inflammatory poems for those lessons.

You: (*uncomfortable and surprised*) Um, okay. I guess I can research poetry form and structure to figure out the best way to help our students analyze the work.

You know immediately that your classroom teacher's decision-making is problematic. The selected poem was written during a highly contentious political moment in United States history. Further, its themes of hope, faith, and resilience are ones that students will be able to identify with, and they also can learn more deeply about the historical and political context that influenced Amanda Gorman's poetry. What should you say? Try using one or more of these sentence starters to draft a response that includes the four ingredients for addressing challenging situations with colleagues.

Affection

- I know you've planned the poetry unit in a really thoughtful way . . .
- I love the idea of using text written by a young poet because . . .
- What a powerful poem you selected . . .

Correction

- I understand that you're concerned about political tensions; however . . .
- We could lay out the factual and historical context by . . .

> ## USE THE FRAMEWORK WITH OTHER STAKEHOLDERS TOO
>
> This process for challenging conversations is something you can use with other school stakeholders, including parents, principals, and administrators. You can also teach the framework, model its use, and guide students to use it in your classroom to have honest and respectful conversations with each other. For additional ideas for how to engage in this work with your students, I highly recommend Janine de Novais' research-based and practical manual, *Brave Community: Teaching for a Post-Racist Imagination* (2023), and Rosalie Rolón-Dow's research on students' experiences with academic microaggressions (2021) and the usefulness of teachers' microaffirmations (2022).

Chapter 4: Embracing Opportunities for Growth

- Teaching the truth is not controversial because . . .
- The themes are . . . so we would need to address . . . to connect to the themes.

Protection

- How do you feel about . . . ?
- Does this make sense . . . ?
- What additional thoughts do you have about . . . ?

Connection

- So for the rest of the poetry unit, we could build on . . .
- Moving forward, maybe we could consider . . .
- I can see these issues coming up again when . . .

To become comfortable using these four elements, Stevenson recommends using multiple forms of practice, including journaling, storytelling, rehearsing, and role-playing. As a participant in one of his multi-day seminars, I learned how to incorporate these practices into my own self-driven professional development. I continue to make mistakes—I'm still learning. There is nothing easy about speaking up and speaking out. You cannot predict how your sentiments will be received by other teachers and colleagues. However, the discomfort you may feel pales in comparison to the harm endured by the students of teachers who are well-intentioned but misguided.

Journal Practice: Redressing Missed Opportunities to Speak Up and Out

There will be moments when you notice something problematic and do not respond. When you start the new school year, your newness may create a deep hesitancy to speak up. You will have rides home where you will chastise yourself and think, "I wish I had said something."

Your silence is not irreparable. You can revisit and reengage with your colleagues. The key to doing this is to strengthen the skills required for it by systematically considering and reimagining the event. No one becomes a better teacher purely by experience; it's reflecting on experience that will enable you to refine, adapt, change, and improve your decision-making and your ability to speak up. The following journal practice will help you build your response skills.

1. Note when you notice a teacher expressing a problematic decision, statement, or behavior. In your journal, describe the event. What are the potential consequences?
2. How did you feel in the past when you experienced similarly stressful encounters? How do you feel now?
3. Describe what you wish you had done in the situation. Explain why you were unable to act.

4. Identify missing information and context. What else do you need to know before you feel you can speak out and up? Seek out these resources and take time to educate yourself. List what you find out and identify which information you will share.
5. Draft a response using the "Redressing Missed Opportunities" form (page 111).
6. Rehearse. You can role-play with a colleague or friend or on your own, using a mirror. You might find it helpful to continue to write in your journal to work through scenarios, which you can revisit and revise.
7. Create a plan for sharing your response. Will you verbally reengage? Send an email? Make a phone call? Will you address it privately, publicly in a meeting, during planning time, in the classroom?

Strategy 20: Make Help-Seeking a Key Part of Your Professional Practice

Over time, help-seeking in classrooms has become normalized. Students are routinely told to ask classmates for help and to approach the teacher if there are points of confusion during a learning activity. Help-seeking by those of us who are supposed to be "experts" is less normalized. Many students and parents see teachers, even first-year teachers, as experts, and many teachers (and other professionals) feel they *should* "know it all," even though they are well aware this is not possible. As a teacher at any stage on the teaching path, it's essential that you seek help whenever you feel you need it.

Co-Teaching: The Huddle

In the teacher preparation program where I work, we use a co-teaching approach to student teaching. On day one of the practicum, candidates and their mentor teachers collaborate to co-plan, co-instruct, and co-evaluate all aspects of teaching and learning. One practice within this model is a huddle (Soslau et al. 2019). Huddles serve as impromptu, brief, real-time meetings during instructional delivery. Huddles are useful because they let you adjust instructional decision-making while teaching. With huddles, new teachers gain expertise in adapting their instruction based on pupil cues, and help-seeking becomes a routine part of teaching.

Rather than keeping all instructional planning confined to lesson co-planning sessions, huddles create additional spaces for teachers to improve their teaching in collaboration with others. Directing pupils to engage in a brain break, think-pair-share, journaling, or some other teacher-free activity opens space for teachers, classroom assistants, co-teachers, and paraprofessionals to converse and strategize with each other during instructional blocks.

Huddles might be used when a classroom teacher notices that students are bored or confused; the teacher can quickly meet with other classroom-based professionals to

Chapter 4: Embracing Opportunities for Growth

brainstorm a change to the planned instructional sequence. A teacher might get stuck explaining a concept and so will call a huddle to seek support. The classroom teacher may also huddle up with support staff who spend time in the classroom, to direct them to check in on students when the teacher needs help supporting diverse learners.

Preparing for Help-Seeking Conversations

It is normal and expected that learners, at any age or experience level, will need help as they develop skills and acquire new knowledge. If you are a student teacher, the practicum is a place for you to be a learner. As a new teacher, you need to continue to learn. Thus, you must be comfortable asking for and receiving help.

To get the type and level of help you need, you can prepare yourself before you reach out. The first step is *preflection*—reflecting on the reasons, possible barriers, and areas for which you want help *before* you reach out to ask for it. The following activity is one you can complete on your own, but it will be more effective if you and a colleague both complete the activity and share the results with each other.

Take your time to think through each of the following preflection questions and record your responses. You want to be prepared to share your ideas with your colleague.

Preflection questions

1. Why would help-seeking—asking questions, requesting advice, sharing challenges, and engaging in collaborative problem-solving—be useful to you and your learning as a teacher?
2. What are some fears or anxieties that might stop you from asking for help?
3. What do you need from your colleague to help alleviate some of your fears and anxieties?
4. What broad areas or topics might you need help with? (lesson planning, classroom environment and culture, building relationships, learning about the community, instructing, assessing, particular disciplines or subject areas)
5. If you need help while you're actively teaching, what would it look like to ask for help? Logistically, how would you get help while you are teaching?
6. What factors might you consider before asking for help? (Can I google it? Is it in the curriculum guide? Is there someone else I should ask before I ask my colleague?)

Bolstered by your own understandings about the help you're seeking, you can then reach out to your colleague for a collegial meeting.

Sample opening script and sentence starters for sharing preflection

"Thank you so much for meeting with me. I want to talk to you about how I can best seek your help and support without placing a burden on you or taking your attention away from our students. Before I ask you a few questions, I want to share some of my own thoughts and feelings about asking for help."

- "First, asking for help can sometimes be difficult for me because . . ."
- "To ease my feelings about this, it would be helpful if . . ."
- "The kind of help I anticipate needing includes . . .
- "If I get stuck and need help during teaching, can we . . ."
- "To ensure that I'm not overburdening you, I plan to do the following things to seek help first . . . Are there other things you'd like me to do?"

Sample questions to ask a mentor teacher or co-teacher
- "Are there certain times where you want help from me and other times when you don't want help? What kind of help would you like from me?"
- "What are the best times throughout the day when I can check in with you for help?"
- "How do you feel about helping me when I'm leading instruction? What might that look like? Should we have a silent signal that we can use to indicate that help is needed?"
- "How do you feel about me helping you when you're leading instruction? What would that look like?"
- "Are there other questions that I should ask you about seeking help or advice or about solving problems collaboratively?"

Your preflection will make it possible for you to reach out confidently for help and to form partnerships with other teachers that can support and enrich your teaching. Getting into the habit of this preflection about the help you need is a skill to maintain throughout your career.

Strategy 21: Embolden Yourself to Contribute Expertise

You want to position yourself as an active contributor; this is your right and your responsibility. As a new teacher, not far away from your teacher preparation programs, you are equipped with current research and evidence-based teaching methods. As more and more teacher preparation programs focus on racial literacy, critical consciousness, multiculturalism, indigenous studies, positive identity development, equity, and justice, teachers new to the workforce are eager and ready to contribute to supporting healthy classroom climates and planning for rigorous, responsive, and sustaining instruction. You may wonder how you can best share your innovative ideas. How can you embolden yourself to contribute ideas during lesson planning, grade team meetings, and other curricular conversations? How can you work to frame your ideas so they will be well received and acted upon?

Chapter 4: Embracing Opportunities for Growth   **103**

AUTHOR SPOTLIGHT

Learning the Hard Way

"I learned the hard way that there are some do's and don'ts for sharing ideas with teacher colleagues. In my first year as a university faculty member, I was working with my field instructor colleagues to revise the student teaching manual. The manual included our syllabus, activities, forms, and directions for the end-of-semester projects. As we worked, I interjected often by pointing out ways we could improve the contents of the manual.

"What I didn't realize was that the way I was speaking and framing my suggestions was hurtful and offensive to my colleagues. Without being aware of it, I bulldozed the activities my colleagues had created, picking apart and finding fault with processes they had established. I succeeded in making a few (thankfully temporary) enemies that day. When the leader of our faculty group privately confided in me that I had offended my colleagues (including herself), I was deeply ashamed. As a result of that experience, I sought and learned more effective ways to present my ideas, in a manner that makes people feel receptive and limits the chance that I would cause harm or make people feel slighted."

Leaning on Brené Brown's work on vulnerability, bell hooks's assertion about the importance of teachers' self-actualization, and Albert Bandura's seminal work on self-efficacy, this section explores why it may be difficult to share your ideas with your teacher colleagues and what you can do about building this crucial collaboration skill.

Vulnerability: Why Is It Hard to Share My Ideas?

Sharing ideas makes us vulnerable. According to Brown (2018), when we share our ideas, we open ourselves to uncertainty, exposure, and risk. We cannot control how someone will interpret what we say or do. Public sharing of ideas puts both our hearts and minds on display. Once our ideas are out there, we risk rejection, humiliation, or being ignored. Human beings are hardwired to avoid pain, which we open ourselves to through our own acts of vulnerability. Thus, vulnerability is difficult.

However, it is also necessary, particularly for teachers who are tasked with continuously collaborating with other professionals, students, families, and communities. As Brown asserts, wholehearted teaching requires vulnerability. So, how do we get comfortable with vulnerability?

Striving Toward Self-Actualization

We know that the more confident we are in ourselves, the more likely we'll step into vulnerability. Here, hooks's (1994) sentiments about the power of self-actualization offer helpful insights. She theorizes that continuously striving toward self-actualization is a grounding feature of how healthy people are and how they move in the world, and she positions self-actualization as a central goal of teaching and learning. A self-actualized teacher is one who knows their value systems, loves themself, extends grace and compassion to themself and others, understands their "why" for teaching, remains open to personal growth, finds pleasure in learning, and has the fortitude to push through discomfort toward the pursuit of educational freedom for all. As opposed to an end point, self-actualization is a process requiring us to align and realign our decision-making to fulfill our own chosen destiny. By the same token, hooks emphasizes the parallel responsibility of teachers to create a context for learning where their students can pursue their pathways to self-actualization.

To remain focused on self-actualization—on the deliberate and systematic push to achieve our own version of our best self—a strong sense of self-efficacy is necessary. What is self-efficacy and why does it matter for teachers?

Growing a Sense of Self-Efficacy

Self-efficacy is the belief that with the right mix of effort and motivation, you can have a positive impact on outcomes for yourself and others. That is, you can achieve whatever it is you set out to accomplish. A teacher's sense of self-efficacy is typified by the belief that they can positively impact their students' learning and well-being. Teachers can build their self-efficacy through self-assessments, experiential learning, positive self-talk and encouragement from others, and strong emotional investment (Bandura 1997).

Bringing It All Together

To build your professional collaborative expertise, you can work to lean into vulnerability, strive for self-actualization, and maintain a strong sense of self-efficacy. Figure 4.1 frames a reflective activity to help you think through how you might attend to these three areas of self-development as you move through the early years of teaching and beyond.

Points of collaboration are opportunities you may have to contribute to your learning community while also building your collaborative expertise. Using one or more of the provided scenarios, or based on your own scenario, consider and write responses to the questions that follow. You may find it helpful to graphically organize your ideas into three columns, or simply use the prompts to guide a reflective journaling session. If you wish, use the "Points of Collaboration Reflection Questions" form (page 112).

Strategy 22: Learn Ways to Manage Stress, Ward Off Burnout, and Find Joy in Teaching

The advice and activities in these pages are not foolproof. A successful reader and doer of this book will still face challenges. Learning to teach is a journey. As cliché as it sounds, it is the truth. On any journey, there will be days, weeks, or even months

Chapter 4: Embracing Opportunities for Growth

Figure 4.1 Points of Collaboration Reflection Questions

Scenarios:

- sharing teaching resources with the grade team
- sharing a self-created resource with your mentor teacher
- talking about a difficult teaching experience or event with your peers
- meeting with the principal to share a concern you have about discipline practices
- asking the reading specialist if you can adjust children's reading group placements

Vulnerability	Self-Actualization	Self-Efficacy
What do I fear most?	In what ways does bringing up my point of collaboration compare or contrast with what I know to be true about teaching and learning?	Describe a similar experience from the past. Was it successful? Why? Was it unsuccessful? Why? Which aspects of my decision-making can I apply to this scenario?
What do I have to reveal about myself/ my thinking?	How will engaging in this point of collaboration bring me closer to the kind of teacher I want to be?	Who can I share my ideas with before I engage in the point of collaboration? What kind of feedback do I need before I proceed?
What am I worried people will judge?	In what ways does this point of collaboration affirm my sense of self as a professional educator?	Why and how will my idea support better teaching and learning? What kind of self-talk can I use to remind myself that I'm working toward an important goal? What mantra might I repeat to myself?
What risks am I taking?	In what ways does taking this risk support my goal to be more authentic to my true self?	A time when I took a risk and it worked out for me was _____. What did I learn about successful risk-taking that could support me now? What other successes can I rely on to boost my sense of control in the current situation?

where you feel disgruntled, stressed, disappointed, dejected—maybe even defeated. This, unfortunately, is the nature of working with other human beings. Further, schools are institutions, often with policies and practices that conflict with your own vision for teaching. Issues from culture, discipline, and assessment to low pay, lack of leadership, and difficult working conditions often lead to teacher burnout.

This information is not secret or new. Likely you've heard of these concerns throughout your teacher preparation program and early days of teaching. So what can you do to manage your stress and ward off burnout? It's essential to prioritize and practice self-care.

There are a range of approaches and methods you can follow to nurture your own well-being. Perform an internet search on managing teacher stress and you will find pages of ideas and resources for relaxation, meditation, mindfulness, deep breathing, exercise, and more. Daily activities like these are critical to well-being, and I urge you to seek out the combination of practices that will sustain you spiritually, physically, and mentally.

Identifying the self-care approaches that work best for you is a helpful prerequisite step to the following section, which highlights four areas of personal and professional support that can ground and enhance your well-being. Each practice can contribute to your ongoing self-care and help you maintain passion and focus on your teaching goals.

Circles of Support at School

Some teacher candidates have been lucky enough to enroll in a teacher preparation program that includes support circles and inquiry groups aimed at sustaining their well-being during student teaching. As a practicing teacher, continuing to engage in opportunities to talk with other teachers and share what you are experiencing and how you're coping will be helpful. I suggest approaching a veteran teacher or the school counselor to see if such support groups already exist at your school site or in your district. If not, you might consider forming your own group.

Professional Counseling

You may feel that you need professional counseling, as many candidates and new teachers do. If so, reach out to find a counselor or therapist who can support you. Your school counselor, nurse, or union representative may be able to connect you to available resources. You might also seek out these resources on your district's or teachers' unions' websites. Non-teaching friends might be able to point you to someone as well. You will likely find online and in-person options for counseling sessions. Talk or email with a counselor you're considering to find out if they feel like a fit for your needs.

A Support Network Beyond School

Support networks include people, resources, or physical spaces. Student teaching can feel stressful, isolating, and overwhelming. If you are nearing the end of your undergraduate studies, many of your peers are engaged in social activities aligned with their final year of college, while you are required to get sleep, wake up early, dress professionally, and show up ready to serve and love the children you will work with. Not only is teaching a demanding enterprise, but you are also entering adulthood and taking on professional responsibilities that your peers are not.

It will be helpful to you to have a support network that you can lean on during challenging times. Similarly, you need to identify people who will celebrate you and your accomplishments during student teaching and through the first few years in your professional role. Think about people who will get it when you describe the demands of the work you are doing and the thrill of achieving something significant.

To begin identifying your support network, consider this question: Who are the people and what are the resources you need to support you so you can engage in the taxing and rewarding work of teaching?

Make a list of people, phone numbers, websites, and organizations to identify resources that are available to you for professional support. Record this information where you can access it easily. Beyond their own immediate communities, many teachers find that professional teacher groups on social media are also helpful places to cultivate relationships and build a network outside their own school.

Rituals of Practice

Teaching well is joyful. I have never encountered a teacher who did not want to experience joy. However, I have met numerous educators who did not know how to cultivate conditions that would elicit joyful feelings. Bringing your whole self into a space and actively nurturing your students' authentic selves through curricular choices and teaching decisions is joyful (Muhammad 2023). Even seemingly mundane and isolating tasks of teaching can be infused with joy through small acts of self-care.

TEACHER SPOTLIGHT

Self-Care

"Having to plan for multiple subjects in elementary was very stressful. It's so important to practice self-care so you don't spiral out of control. You have to take care of yourself before you can be capable of taking care of others. My school is big on self-care and mindfulness. Our students practice mindful breathing every day with the morning announcements so they know what to do when they are experiencing stress. This daily practice is good for all of us, staff and students alike."

Many artists and writers engage in rituals of practice that enable them to be physically and mentally prepared to joyfully complete tasks. For example, when I prepare to write, I make sure my desk is clean, I burn a particular scented incense, I listen to relaxing music, and I make sure I have a refreshing drink and yummy snack on hand. When I read academic journals or books, I light a candle, sit in a particular reading chair, curl up with a cozy blanket, and ensure my family knows to leave me alone. I look forward to these tasks because they feel luxurious. Time to myself, stretching my mind or being creative, is pleasurable.

Even small acts can have a positive impact. Your ritual does not need to be elaborate. For example, I have a colleague who keeps fuzzy slippers tucked in a desk drawer in her classroom. During her solitary preparation time, she wears her "cozy shoes."

The main idea here is that rituals can make a required and daunting task feel joyful. Think about the tasks you are called to do in teaching—grading papers, creating lesson plans, completing course assignments, and so on. How can you add joy to these tasks? Think about where you want to be when you do each task. What do you want to smell and hear? What setting or conditions can you arrange for yourself so that completing the task brings you joy?

The "My Plan for Joyful Task Completion" form (page 113) will help you plan for ways you can maintain your well-being as you engage in the taxing work of learning to teach and growing in your profession.

Read through the following questions and plot out your plan, using the form or your journal and noting times and activities on a digital calendar or your own planner. Consider sharing your plan with a peer or someone in your support network. Together you can hold each other accountable for your self-care plans.

Daily. What daily practices can you implement to center yourself before the day, at midday, and at the end of the day? What can you do to support your physical and emotional health each day? What times and days will you complete these practices?

Weekly. What special activities can you look forward to each week (phone calls with family and friends, music, events, reading for pleasure, working out, meals, movies, and so on)? Be sure to include a special activity each week in your calendar. If you can do more than one thing, even better!

Monthly. How can you mark your achievements, progress, and accomplishments in teaching? What monthly celebratory ritual can you create for yourself? Do you want to celebrate privately, or with others? Which people in your life would want to hear about your good news from the field?

REALITY CHECK: WHAT'S IN YOUR CONTROL?

Over the years, I have written about ways that teacher candidates can manage their own professional, teacher-related emotional needs (Soslau 2015a, 2015b; Soslau and Alexander 2021). These include reasonable emotional needs such as a sense of belonging in the classroom. However, some needs, such as the need to feel in control at all times, can harm teachers. I urge you to think about your locus of control. What can you impact and what can you *not* impact? If you spend time, energy, and emotional bandwidth on aspects of teaching and learning that you cannot impact, then you are setting yourself up for increasing stress and self-defeat. Instead, practice setting aside what you cannot control and focusing your efforts on the many aspects of teaching where you can enact improvements. Relishing in the pursuit of making a meaningful difference with your teaching will enable you to find satisfaction and joy in your work.

Chapter 4: Embracing Opportunities for Growth

• • •

This chapter helped you predict and navigate challenges while identifying opportunities to develop your collaborative expertise. You now have concrete strategies and actions for:

- addressing problematic decision-making, utterances, or behaviors exhibited by other professionals
- embracing and engaging in help-seeking processes
- contributing your own expertise
- building your tolerance for vulnerability, becoming self-actualized, and boosting self-efficacy
- bringing joy to required tasks
- supporting and maintaining your emotional-well being

Redressing Missed Opportunities

Original Scenario

Affection	Correction	Connection	Protection

New Response

When You're the New Teacher: 28 Strategies to Align Your Good Intentions with Your Teaching Practices
© Elizabeth Soslau—Free Spirit Publishing

Points of Collaboration Reflection Questions

Scenario(s):

Vulnerability	Self-Actualization	Self-Efficacy
What do I fear most?	In what ways does bringing up my point of collaboration compare or contrast with what I know to be true about teaching and learning?	Describe a similar experience from the past. Was it successful? Why? Was it unsuccessful? Why? Which aspects of my decision-making can I apply to this scenario?
What do I have to reveal about myself/my thinking?	How will the act of engaging in this point of collaboration bring me closer to the kind of teacher I want to be?	Who can I share my ideas with before I engage in the point of collaboration? What kind of feedback do I need before I proceed?
What am I worried people will judge?	In what ways does this point of collaboration affirm my sense of self as a professional educator?	Why and how will my idea support better teaching and learning? What kind of self-talk can I use to remind myself that I'm working toward an important goal? What mantra might I repeat to myself?
What risks am I taking?	In what ways does taking this risk support my goal to be more authentic to my true self?	A time when I took a risk and it worked out for me was _____. What did I learn about successful risk-taking that could support me now? What other successes can I rely on to boost my sense of control in the current situation?

When You're the New Teacher: 28 Strategies to Align Your Good Intentions with Your Teaching Practices
© Elizabeth Soslau—Free Spirit Publishing

My Plan for Joyful Task Completion

Task	Where do I want to be?	What do I want to smell?	What do I want to hear?	What do I want to feel?	What other conditions do I want to create?
Lesson Planning					
Grading Papers					
Reading/ Researching					

When You're the New Teacher: 28 Strategies to Align Your Good Intentions with Your Teaching Practices

© Elizabeth Soslau—Free Spirit Publishing

Moving Out and Beyond

Strategies for Transitioning to a New Classroom, School, or Role

Teachers experience many transitions in their professional lifespans. Teacher candidates leave practicum placements, new teachers embark on their first year of teaching, and teachers at any career stage find themselves in new grade levels, new schools, and new districts. These transitions do not have to produce anxiety! With careful planning, you can smoothly move through these changes and lay the groundwork for a productive entry into a new educational context.

In this chapter you will find support and resources to help you answer these questions:

- How can I work through my feelings and say a thoughtful goodbye?
- How can I track my accomplishments and build my teaching portfolio?
- How can I learn about my new curriculum?
- What are my goals for my teaching and my students in the year ahead?
- How will I arrange my new teaching space?
- What professional learning and development will help me be ready for my new role?

Transitions are a natural part of teaching. Even if an upcoming change is your choice, moving on can make you feel unmoored. Taking action can guide you into feeling more settled. As you journey forward in your career, try to maintain an adaptive mindset. With an approach that's both deliberative and active, you can do this with confidence. This chapter offers practical and reflective strategies to help you transition from your current role to the next stage in your career.

TEACHER SPOTLIGHT

Transitions

"I have switched schools and grade levels and positions a lot. Most people hear my story of all the changes in my first ten years of teaching and feel sorry for me. I'm glad I went through so many changes early in my teaching career, because it shaped and molded me into the teacher I am today. I have learned so much from each school and grade level and have made lots of long-lasting friendships too. Each time I find out my position is changing, I look at the positive: I still have a job and I'm excited to learn something new. I enjoy taking on new challenges because it helps me grow, provides new experiences, and takes me out of my comfort zone."

• • •

"I started out at a city school teaching middle school science for two years. Then I taught second grade at a private day school for three years—and then spent two months as their middle school science teacher before moving to my current position. The hardest move was leaving mid-year. I wrote a speech to read to the kids, and I was crying and shaking when I read it because I really do love the kids I teach, no matter where I am."

Strategy 23: Reflect and Plan to Make Goodbyes Meaningful

When you learn that you must leave your students, colleagues, or school community, it is reasonable to be sad and feel some trepidation about what lies ahead.

One way to move through the sadness is to take time to explore what you're feeling and plan how you'll say goodbye. To guide yourself in this process, use your journal to reflect and write about prompts like the following.

As I look toward the end of the school year,

- I am looking forward to . . .
- I feel trepidation about . . .
- I am anxious for . . .
- I feel energized about . . .

As I think about saying goodbye to my students and colleagues,

- I am worried that . . .
- I am heartened by . . .
- I think I will feel . . .
- I want them to know . . .

116 When You're the New Teacher

After responding to the prompts, you can further clarify your thoughts and emotions with a 3-2-1 summary:

3 things I'll miss the most are . . .
2 people I want to remain connected to are . . .
1 memory or lesson I learned that I'll carry with me is . . .

Once you have dedicated some time to processing your feelings, consider how you will say goodbye to the students and colleagues that you've worked closely with over the school year. Some teachers write letters to their students, host a picnic at a local park, plan a social hour with colleagues, or create video messages to be shared with students and their families. Part of these intentional goodbyes might include sharing your feelings toward your students and colleagues and the special memories you'll carry with you.

TEACHER SPOTLIGHT

Meaningful Goodbyes

"Since I began teaching several years ago, I have written a note for each student at the end of the school year. The tradition began as a way for me to reflect on the school year and acknowledge the growth of each student individually. I wrote every card with the intent of discussing them as a person rather than emphasizing their academics throughout the year. I wanted to ensure that each student realized I saw them as a person who is growing, and not just a student with academic successes and failures.

"For the first couple of years, my students took the cards, read them, and said thank you. They went about their lives. About six years into teaching, I received two separate emails about the cards. One was from a former student who said she appreciated that I'd recognized that she had a tough, emotional year as an eighth grader. She kept the card in her room and used it to motivate herself to go to college. The student told me that she was now pursuing teaching and thanked me for the inspiration.

"The other email was from the mother of a former student, who wrote that her son had been in and out of mental health facilities for suicidal ideation. The parents had been clearing out the student's room to help create a fresh start when they found the card I had given him at the end of ninth grade. This mom wanted me to know that the young man smiled and asked to keep the card.

"Although the cards are just pieces of paper, some of them stayed with students and highlighted our positive relationship. I was glad I'd been able to support students' social and emotional well-being."

Chapter 5: Moving Out and Beyond

Strategy 24: Expand Your Portfolio

It's wise to be growing your portfolio and adding artifacts each year that you're in the field, even if your position doesn't change. For example, you might take photos of your students working on a collaborative project, make copies of a few student work products, and print a copy of a unit that you developed independently. Add the items to your teaching portfolio to share during future job interviews. They will serve as compelling visual aids as you talk about your professional accomplishments.

Moving on in your teaching career provides a timely opportunity to ask the people in your current school to provide you with evidence of your excellence in teaching, which you can add to your teaching portfolio. Three important types of portfolio pieces that you can gather as evidence of your professional growth and teaching excellence are peer reports, administrative reports, and letters of recommendation. While you can of course ask for peer and administrative feedback reports at any time, you are most likely to ask for a letter of recommendation when you are thinking about moving on to a new position.

Peer Reports

Your colleagues are often the people who can share insight about your teaching practice. Chapter 2 included a simple "Peer Observation Form" (page 65) to use for ongoing feedback and coaching.

A second and more formal method is to request peer observation reports intended to provide evidence of your skills in planning, instruction, forming a positive classroom climate, and assessment. Your peers are well positioned to observe a lesson and write a report about how you organize instructional procedures, select materials, and align your classroom activities to lesson goals and assessments (planning). Further, they have the expertise to comment on the implementation of your plans (instruction) and the ways in which you create a learning environment conducive to student success (classroom climate). Finally, peers can observe and comment on your data collection approaches and discern the usefulness of your assessments to accurately capture what your students learned and understand. These peer reports can become important portfolio pieces that you can share with future employers.

Carefully think about which peer reports or feedback forms you want to include in your portfolio. For example, if the peer feedback form from chapter 2 is glowing and highlights your skills, you will want to include it. However, remember that the original purpose of that peer feedback form was to collect data to improve your teaching. Thus, your peer may have shared critical feedback that you would not want to include in your portfolio. On the other hand, your peer may have helped you identify an area of your practice for improvement, which you then successfully strengthened. Documenting your process of seeking feedback and improving your practice could be a powerful artifact for your portfolio. The takeaway idea here is to be strategic: have a clear rationale and be discerning when choosing what to include.

For a formal peer report, you will need to direct the observation by providing explicit instructions about which aspects of your instruction are to be the focus. Consider providing your peer observer with an observation report form that is easy to complete and, equally important, can be read and digested quickly by future employers. If you wish, use the "Peer Report" form (page 127), adapt the form to suit your needs, or let it serve as a model for you to create your own form. If you teach multiple subjects or grade levels, consider having a different peer observe each subject-area and grade-level lesson to write a report.

Administrator Reports

In many instances, school administrators will regularly observe your teaching and provide you with written feedback. You might decide to include these reports in your portfolio, or you might ask your principal to create a report that specifically highlights your talents and professional expertise. While your administrator can certainly write a report using the same categories as your peer reviewer, administrators can also speak to your professionalism and leadership skills. In either case, most future employers will be eager to access administrator-level feedback about your teaching. Consider providing your administrator with a copy of the "Administrator Report" form on page 129 and sharing the example of report details in figure 5.1. While you need to be open to your administrator's desire to create or use their own template, be sure to clearly communicate that you are seeking a report that you will be sharing with potential future employers.

Figure 5.1 Sample Administrator Report Details

	Planning	Instruction	Assessment	Professionalism	Leadership
Strengths	Detailed and thoughtful lesson plans, demonstrates creativity.	Keen focus on differentiated approaches to reach all students.	Assessments are aligned to objectives and are tiered for students' needs.	Timely, mature, conscientious, works and communicates well with parents.	Chaired the DEI committee and led the grade team in PBL initiative.
Growth Areas	Plan ways to quickly assess prior knowledge to unearth misconceptions.	Continue to ask higher-order thinking questions.	Use prior assessments to plan for remediation or acceleration.	N/A	Consider taking on positions such as grade team leader or department chair.

Letters of Recommendation

In addition to feedback forms or observation reports, you may need or want to solicit letters of recommendation. It's important to ensure that the letters focus on your professional connection to the letter writers as opposed to any personal relationships you may have with them. As a letter writer for many of my former preservice teachers,

I often request that the teacher-applicant send me their résumé as well as a set of bullet points and highlights that I can address in my letter. You will greatly increase the chances of receiving a strong letter of recommendation if you follow these steps.

1. Provide a clear deadline for when you need the letter.
   "Thank you so much for considering writing a letter of recommendation for me. If you decide to write the letter, can you please send me a copy by July 2?"

2. Attach your résumé to your request.
   "Please find my résumé attached. You will notice that I have included special commendations and teaching awards, which you might decide to mention in your letter."

3. Include bullets that describe your strengths and any accomplishments.
   "My teaching strengths include . . . I am also proud of . . . This past year I was able to . . ."

4. Offer to meet for a brief chat to discuss what you hope the letter writer will include.
   "I'm available to meet to discuss any questions you might have about writing the letter."

Portfolio Planning

Use a tracking form to ensure you can collect all documentation before you plan to move to a new position. Figure 5.2 is an example of a simple tracking form.

Figure 5.2 Sample Portfolio Tracking Form

	Who?	Format?	Date Requested	Date Received
Peer reports	• grade team leader • department chair • partner teacher	form provided	April 25	April 28
Administrator reports	• academic dean • instructional coach	form provided	March 18	
Letters of recommendation	• principal • regional superintendent	letter	May 2	
Work samples	• students	"Animal Project" essays (redacted)	January 9	January 9
Photos of community clean-up	• school photographer	electronic images	April 14	

Strategy 25: Prepare for New Beginnings

No matter when you find out that a professional transition is on the horizon, there are steps you can take to prepare for your new educational context. In chapter 1, you explored ideas to get to know your students, families, and the community assets available to you. This section and the planning document provided at the conclusion of this chapter will help you build on the activities from chapter 1. Specifically, the aim of this chapter is to support you as you prepare for another successful school year in a new context by becoming familiar with your new curriculum, beginning to plan your classroom layout, and generating ideas for what you can do in the summer to continue your professional development.

Early Relationship Building

Once you secure your next teaching position, get to know your new colleagues as soon as possible. One way of doing this is researching the school's website to find names and contact details of folks whom you are likely to work with. For example, if you'll be teaching third grade, you might send an email introducing yourself to all the third grade teachers. For a high school position, you might contact the history department chair to introduce yourself as the new tenth grade ancient civilizations teacher. If you can't find contact details on the school's website, send an email to the principal or the principal's administrative assistant to request them.

Reaching out to the teachers' union, or to school- or district-level human services representatives, can help you discover existing social networks or supports for new teachers or teachers new to the school. Many districts have induction programs to support new teachers. These programs serve several functions, including orientation to the district and school, arranging for mentorship and support, new teacher workshops, and social gatherings. Reach out early and often to seek these connections. Even if you do not receive a response immediately, you'll be on people's radar as someone who is eager to build professional relationships.

Curriculum Investigation

Becoming familiar with the curriculum materials that you're required to use will help you enter the new school year with a higher sense of confidence. Most schools have dedicated staff to oversee curriculum selection and implementation. Often, these staff members are content area experts or coaches. Using your school's website to identify the right point person, reach out and request information about the curriculum that you will be expected to use in the coming school year. If this person is unavailable to you, contact the district curriculum office, which is usually fully staffed throughout the summer months.

Some things you might seek access to include:

- state/district required standards and benchmark testing schedules
- links to online curricular components and resources
- teacher manuals
- a set of student materials (readers, workbooks, and so forth)
- supplemental software or online training programs
- dates and locations for curriculum training offered by publishers or the district

Once you receive the curriculum materials, consider these questions to make sense of the resources.

1. What state/district standards do I need to adhere to when planning for the school year?
2. What is the assessment schedule for my content area/grade level?
3. What is the curricular scope and sequence for my content area/grade level?
4. What texts are required?
5. What other requirements are nonnegotiable?
6. How much noninstructional time will I have at the start of the year for community building?
7. Are resources for differentiation available?
8. Who are the point people to approach for curriculum-related questions? What is the best way to get in touch with them?

Strategy 26: Set Yearlong Aspirations for Curriculum and Learning

Once you know what the required curriculum looks like, you can think about what *you* want for your students in the coming year. In my work with preservice and in-service teachers, I consistently express the same refrain: "The curriculum writers never met *your* students, nor are they teaching at *your* school in the *current* social climate." The curriculum you have been provided represents the developers' and authors' best understanding of what is going to be appropriate, relevant, useful, and exciting for your students. Yet you work in a specific place, at a specific time, with specific students. While you certainly need to be attentive to the curricular requirements and standards, you also need to flex your professional expertise. You earned a teaching degree and most likely hold a teaching credential or certification. You are equipped to think through learning goals that matter to *your* students.

So, what will it be? What are the big ideas you want your students to wrestle with this school year? What questions do you hope they can answer and what takeaways do you want them to bring forward when their educational journey moves beyond your classroom at the close of the school year?

These are exciting—and perhaps overwhelming—things to ponder as a new *or* experienced teacher. The following journal activity is designed to help you puzzle through these ideas in a manageable progression, thinking about students' learning goals and how to address them using *what, how, who,* and *why* questions.

A Wish List of Student Learning Goals

To begin, imagine that anything is possible, there are no time constraints, no budget concerns, no binding parameters. What big questions or takeaways do you want your students to explore this year? Writing as freely as you can, make a wish list of student learning goals.

Journal Reflection about the Goals

When you've finished, read and answer three sets of questions, revising your goals as you go.

What questions

1. What might my students already know about these learning goals from earlier grade levels?
2. In what ways are the big questions or takeaways tied to my required curricular components?
3. What additional resources do I need to identify to supplement what is provided?
4. What curricular flexibility do I have to incorporate these needs in my learning goals?

Stay in freewriting mode as you revise your list of student learning goals.

How questions

1. How can I provide a variety of experiential learning opportunities?
2. How can I educate myself in order to implement these learning goals?

Continue to freely revise the list of learning goals.

Who questions

1. Whom do I need to contact for permission?
2. Whom might I collaborate with on these learning goals?

Continue to freely revise the list of learning goals.

Why questions

1. Why do these learning goals matter to my students, their families, and their communities?
2. Why do these learning goals matter to me?
3. Why and how are these learning goals useful and meaningful to my students?

Revise the list of learning goals.

Chapter 5: Moving Out and Beyond   **123**

Next Steps

At the conclusion of this task, you will have a list of learning goals, essential questions, or aims that you want to address during the upcoming school year. To be sure, as you prepare for your transition into your new teaching position, these ideas may shift, grow, or move to the background. That is okay. The planning and visioning process now can still serve as an energizing activity as you embark on the new school year, one that can evolve and even help ground you as you get to know your new students.

Some of your learning goals may be aspirational. Your students may begin on a learning trajectory toward a particular understanding, but might not fully master the concepts or ideas. Or there may be an instructional approach that you need to try out or curriculum material you want to include but are not yet able to do so because of circumstances beyond your control. When this happens, it is helpful to think about these aspirational ideas as future doorways that you can still walk toward.

Taking smaller steps now can help you fully realize these aspirations in the future. For example, you may want to implement a guest speaker series because one of your learning goals is for students to have authentic, real-life examples to draw from when developing their understanding of a particular concept or topic. However, you quickly learn that you need many months to plan such a series. A small step toward this aspirational goal is to spend some time curating a list of guest speakers. You can still introduce these experts and professionals by sharing your research and curated list with your students. You may not have implemented your plan to bring in guest speakers, but you are gathering necessary information that can help you provide your administration with a compelling rationale for future school years.

Strategy 27: Visit and Start Planning for Your New Space

No matter where you teach, the space you teach in matters. Ask your new administrator if a tour of the building is part of your onboarding process before the school year begins. If it's not, ask if you can visit the school over the summer and see your classroom. Once there, take photos and measurements. This might seem excessive, but it isn't. How you lay out your classroom will communicate to your students how you expect them to behave and interact with one another.

There are many ways you can configure your teaching space. You might decide to get rid of the teacher desk (a popular decision in a charter school I taught at), or you might decide to put your desk right up front where all the students can see you. Desks in rows will prompt different expectations than desks configured in collaborative clumps or in a circle. Do you want your students to have easy access to each other for partner work, or is it important that everyone in the classroom can always see each other? Many teachers will also reconfigure the furniture depending on the lesson. Think through what you want your students to see when they walk into your classroom on the very first day. You can always adjust from there.

You might also find it useful to talk to other teachers about how they arrange their classrooms. Probe for the *why* behind their decision-making. Why desks in groups of four and not six? Why get rid of the teacher's desk? Why are some seats chairs while others are large, inflated balls?

The power of talking to other teachers cannot be overstated. I picked up one of my favorite classroom design decisions from a special education teacher. I had configured my classroom in a horseshoe shape with the opening of the "U" facing the board in the front of the room. I shared with my colleague that I was nervous about turning my back on my class. My students were wonderfully creative, and they found ingenious ways to entertain themselves when I wasn't looking. Often, I found myself wishing I had eyes in the back of my head. I mentioned this during lunch break one day and the special educator told me to get a cheap, lightweight, full-length mirror and hang it horizontally above my whiteboard. This way I could use it like a rearview mirror. Genius! I never taught without a rearview mirror again.

Strategy 28: Make Time for Summer Learning

Every teacher deserves to relax and enter a period of renewal over the summer. Teachers routinely put in over fifty hours of work per week (Najarro 2022). Many full-time classroom teachers find themselves working late into the evenings and on weekends. When summer finally arrives, teachers are exhausted and drained. On top of that, teachers preparing for new positions need to dedicate time to make a smooth transition to their new role. With all that you have on your plate already, you may wonder why I'm recommending that you also make it a priority to engage in summer scholarship—and how you can carve out time to do this while still allowing yourself needed R & R.

Summer learning is critical for two reasons: The first is that teachers have very little time to read during the school year; summer presents opportunities to carve out time and focus on a topic of interest. Second, many teachers wish to improve on something from the previous school year. For these reasons, I urge teachers to take time over the summer to read at least two books or articles or access other professional resources such as free webinars, online workshops, and podcasts to get new ideas for the next school year.

Draw from the prompts below to identify topics of interest you want to investigate over the summer.

- I would like more ideas about how to teach . . .
- I need a better way to teach about . . .
- I wish I could help students in my class with . . .
- When students ask questions about . . . I wish I knew more about . . .
- The aspect of relationship building I need to work on is . . .
- I can make my classroom more inclusive, but first I need to know . . .

- I wish I knew more about . . .
- Next year for our faculty inquiry group, I'd like to work on . . .
- I really struggled with . . . this past year.
- Big questions I have about education are . . .
- I need more ideas about how to address . . .

You might find that you want to learn more about teaching philosophy or theory rather than focus on how to improve on a particular instructional approach. Or you might decide that you really want to work on different ways to teach a particular mathematics concept. No matter what, challenge yourself to learn two new things from the professional resources that you choose to explore. Feel good about taking personal initiative to improve your practice and widen your knowledge base. Ask your teacher peers to join you in your pursuit of summer scholarship. You might even suggest they read this book!

• • •

This chapter helped you think through the inevitable transitions that await you throughout your professional career. You now have concrete strategies and actions for:

- processing your feelings about moving on at the conclusion of the school year
- building your teaching portfolio with peer and administrator reports and letters of recommendation
- investigating your new curriculum and setting aspirations for students' learning
- planning your physical space
- selecting professional materials for summer scholarship

Peer Report

Teacher Name: _____   **Date:** _____

Content Area: _____   **Grade Level:** _____

Lesson Focus/Objective/Goals:

Classroom Climate: Mark an **X** on the continuum.

Peaceful ⟨——————————————————————⟩ Chaotic

Highly Engaged ⟨——————————————————⟩ Low Engagement

Collaborative ⟨——————————————————⟩ Individualized

Clear Expectations ⟨————————————————⟩ Disorganized Expectations

Classroom Climate Comments:

Instructional Decision-Making: Mark an **X** on the continuum.

Objectives & Assessment Well Aligned ⟨————————⟩ Weak Alignment

Clearly Modeled Concepts ⟨————————————————⟩ No Modeling

Strong Questioning Techniques ⟨————————————⟩ Limited Questioning

Addresses Students' Needs ⟨————————————————⟩ No Differentiation

Instructional Decision-Making Comments:

(continued on next page)

(continued from previous page)

Assessment: Based on all available data (observation, pupil oral responses, worksheets, group discussions, and so on), circle "Yes" or "No."

Assessments are aligned to learning goals.   Yes   No

Checks for understanding occurred throughout the lesson.   Yes   No

Individual assessment data is collected for each student.   Yes   No

Data represents what students understand or are able to do.   Yes   No

Data is useful for supporting future instructional decisions.   Yes   No

Assessment data can be used as feedback for students to further develop their thinking or work product.   Yes   No

Assessment Comments:
(Please be sure to explain each "No" answer.)

Other Comments:

Administrator Report

Teacher Name: _____ **Academic Year(s):** _____

Grade Level: _____ **Subject(s):** _____

	Planning	Instruction	Assessment	Professionalism	Leadership
Strengths					
Growth Areas					

When You're the New Teacher: 28 Strategies to Align Your Good Intentions with Your Teaching Practices

© Elizabeth Soslau—Free Spirit Publishing

Portfolio Tracking Form

	Who?	Format?	Date Requested	Date Received
Peer reports				
Administrator reports				
Letters of Recommendation				

When You're the New Teacher: 28 Strategies to Align Your Good Intentions with Your Teaching Practices

© Elizabeth Soslau—Free Spirit Publishing

A Final Word of Encouragement

All teachers enter their teaching career with clear ideas about teaching practices and decision-making that they think will be beneficial for their students. Like many new teachers, you may be looking ahead with excitement and aspiration. You may intend to humanize your teaching, to elevate community assets and family wisdom, to put students at the center of all that you do, to stand up and speak out, to be collaborative—to do it all! Yet all teachers face challenges and obstacles. Sometimes these challenges and obstacles knock us off our intended course. Our practice no longer reflects all our initial good intentions. This is known as an intention-behavior gap. Using the strategies and approaches in this book can help you get back on course and steadily close that gap.

My wish for you is that your classroom is a space where you and your students can be their whole selves. I want you to be able to reflect on each day, week, month, and academic year with pride, knowing you did all you could to do right by your students. When you were unsure, you sought help. When you made mistakes, you learned from them, educated yourself, and committed to doing better. And when you bumped up against something that made you question, forget, or abandon your intentions, you paused and asked, "Is this good for my students?"

Ignite, rekindle, and continuously stoke your passion for serving your students well—and you will make good on your good intentions.

Acknowledgments

Like many of my accomplishments, the genesis of this book was the result of a serendipitous encounter. One of my colleagues, Jill Flynn, told her friend Tom Rademacher (acquisitions editor for Free Spirit) about my work. Introductions were made, conversations ensued, and voilà—you're holding this book. Thank you to Jill for trumpeting me and my work. And thank you to Tom for taking a chance on me.

During a 2023 New Year's dinner with two treasured colleagues and friends, Rosalie Rolón-Dow and Janine de Novais, we set intentions for the coming year. This book was one of my intentions. Fast-forward to our 2024 New Year's meal, where Janine pulled out a small journal, which Rosalie had gifted each of us, and proceeded to read our 2023 intentions aloud. I basked in their joy for me as I was able to report my progress on this book. Thank you, Rosalie and Janine, for always telling me that my ideas matter.

Writing the book was fun; working with my editor was even better. Margie Lisovskis is a phenomenal editor and a brilliant thought partner. She is kind, efficient, smart—and her efforts made my book so much better. Thank you, Margie.

Readers will undoubtably appreciate the wisdom offered by the fabulous teachers, administrators, and students who contributed to this book. I am deeply grateful for the sentiments these folks generously shared so that we could all learn from their experiences.

A big shout out to:

School administrators Jaela Hall-Russell and Erik Jones. Jaela, your insights have always been valuable to me. I thank you for sharing your wisdom with my readers. Your friendship means more to me than you will ever know. Erik, you've always made time for guest lectures, and I am forever grateful.

Teachers Laura Behrens, Michelle Bernardi, Alexis Bigelow, Amanda Cahill, Emily Herbstritt, Olivia Linder, Tasha Moore, Denise Rogers, David Soslau, Arielle Starkman, and Leah Wright. Michelle, your insights about your relationship with your principal are so helpful. Alexis, your story about Black History Month and your collaboration with a parent was such a powerful contribution to this book. Amanda, learning about the impact of your handwritten notes to students will surely inspire readers to do the same. Emily, Tasha, and Leah, I'm so glad to be able to call you colleagues, and friends. Your anecdotes about starting fresh and starting over will undoubtedly help new and veteran teachers alike. Denise, your story about Kelly Wreath, may she rest in peace, is both compelling and instructive. I hope that readers will feel as touched as I do by your addition to this text. David, it isn't easy to share stories about professional self-improvement efforts. Thank you for making it okay to make mistakes. Laura, Olivia, and Arielle, thank you so much for taking time out of your busy teaching lives to contribute to this text. You all made the book so much richer. Thank you, thank you, thank you!

Students Ella, Harry, Ryan C., Ryan K., Yaya, Julian, and Jake. Yaya, Ella, and Ryan K., thank you for contributing your voices as "big" kids. I love what you shared about the importance of teachers' kindness, even in high school settings. Ryan C., I'm so glad that your mathematics teacher took you under her wing. Harry, my love, thank you for helping me with my book. Julian, your video message about the importance of teachers calling on you was such an important point. Jake, thank you so much for reminding us all how important it is for a teacher to care about children as *people*, not just as students. I couldn't agree more. Thanks and love to all of you for sharing your student voices with my readers and with me. And parents—Christie Blair, Larry Wachtel Cohen, Sandra Cook, Chris Counter, Marcie Soslau Johnson, Rachel Karchmer-Klein, and Terri Ozoroski—thank you for the behind-the-scenes logistics to coordinate the video messages, text messages, audio files, and permission forms.

Most of the scenarios and stories in this book have happened to me, or to my students. I want to thank the fall 2023 doctoral students from our Culturally Responsive Pedagogy course for the idea for one of the stories. You'll know which one.

Finally, I thank my family and friends for their love and support. No matter what, they are always proud of me and think that what I do is important. I carry their pride, love, and value for me in my soul. I love you all, forever. xox

Appendix

Expert Perspectives: Foundations for Teaching and Learning

Throughout this book, I share the wisdom of educational experts. Following are brief biographies of each of these individuals.

Albert Bandura was professor emeritus at Stanford University and former president of the American Psychological Association. He is considered the grandfather of social cognitive theory. His research has influenced teachers to use instructional practices that support self-regulation and self-efficacy building. His experimental work on modeling is one of his most impactful contributions in education.

Brené Brown is a professor at the University of Houston's graduate college of social work. Her research focuses on courage, vulnerability, shame, and empathy. She is the author of several books, including *The Gifts of Imperfection* and *Atlas of the Heart*, and hosts two podcasts: *Unlocking Us* and *Dare to Lead*.

Joyce Epstein, professor of education at Johns Hopkins University, is best known for her research on the power of family engagement in schools. She emphasizes the importance of including families as school partners. Her research has shown the positive impact of family involvement on student achievement.

bell hooks was a feminist philosopher, scholar, and author of numerous books. In *Teaching to Transgress*, hooks argues that teaching should be inclusive and egalitarian and encourage critical thinking, urging teachers to bring their whole selves into the classroom and to encourage their students to do the same. She also reminds educators that while storytelling and personal lived experiences are important, these ideas are truly relevant when teachers and learners can connect the experiences to academic content through rigorous, scholarly, and collaborative work.

Gloria Ladson-Billings, professor emerita at the University of Wisconsin–Madison, is best known for her work on culturally relevant teaching, and more recently her work on the role of critical race theory in education. She has written extensively on the importance of incorporating students' cultural backgrounds into the curriculum and on critical consciousness raising as a learning outcome. Her work shifted rhetoric about the achievement gap to the more apt phrase *opportunity gap*, which places a spotlight on systemic inequality in schooling and its oppressive impact on children of color.

Bettina Love is an associate professor of education at the University of Georgia and author of *We Want to Do More Than Survive: Abolitionist Teaching and the Pursuit of Educational Freedom* and *Punished for Dreaming: How School Reform Harms Black Children and How We Heal.* She is also the co-founder of the Abolitionist Teaching Network. Her work centers humanism and love within abolitionist teaching approaches and learning outcomes.

Karen Mapp, professor at the Harvard Graduate School of Education, developed a well-cited framework for guiding family-school partnerships. She emphasizes the critical need to build relationships through the development of deep trust and respect.

Robert Marzano is a prolific author of over fifty books. As part of his work with the Learning Sciences Marzano Center, he has developed frameworks for classroom instruction, teacher evaluation, and leadership development. Notably, his work on the usefulness of teacher collaboration and peer coaching has inspired decades of work in schools where teachers support each other in their own professional development.

Luis Moll, professor emeritus at the University of Arizona, conducts research on the ways in which culture and language influence teaching and learning. He is most known for his work developing the sociocultural theory named *Funds of Knowledge.* His work focuses on the importance of recognizing and valuing students' cultural backgrounds in the classroom as valid ways of knowing.

Gholnecsar (Gholdy) Muhammad is an associate professor at Georgia State University and author of *Cultivating Genius: An Equity Framework for Culturally and Historically Responsive Literacy* and *Unearthing Joy: A Guide to Culturally and Historically Responsive Curriculum and Instruction.* Her work has been instrumental in focusing the power of literacy instruction toward the goal of cultivating positive identity development, critical thinking, and intellectual rigor.

Nell Noddings was professor emerita at Stanford University. She is best remembered for her work on the philosophy of education and ethics of care. Her work started a movement that encouraged educators to view caring as an essential and critical component of instructional practice in preK–12 schools and beyond.

Howard Stevenson is a professor of urban education, human development, quantitative methods, and Africana studies at the University of Pennsylvania. He is also the director of the Racial Empowerment Collaborative and founder of the Lion's Story. He is a nationally renowned speaker and prolific scholar. His book *Promoting Racial Literacy in Schools: Differences That Make a Difference* has become an essential text for educators who want to learn and teach how to identify, manage, and resolve racially stressful encounters.

References

Bandura, Albert. 1997. *Self-Efficacy: The Exercise of Control*. New York: W. H. Freeman and Company.

Bishop, Rudine Sims. 1990. "Mirrors, Windows, and Sliding Glass Doors." *Perspectives: Choosing and Using Books for the Classroom* 6 (3).

Brown, Brené. 2018. *Dare to Lead: Brave Work. Tough Conversations. Whole Hearts*. New York: Random House.

De Novais, Janine. 2023. *Brave Community: Teaching for a Post-Racist Imagination*. New York: Teachers College Press.

Epstein, Joyce L., Mavis G. Sanders, Steven Sheldon, Beth S. Simon, Karen Clark Salinas, Natalie R. Jansorn, Frances L. VanVoorhis, Cecelia S. Martin, Brenda G. Thomas, Marsha D. Greenfield, Darcy J. Hutchins, and Kenyatta J. Williams. 2019. *School, Family, and Community Partnerships: Your Handbook for Action, Fourth Edition*, and *Handbook CD*. Thousand Oaks CA: Corwin. See www.partnershipschools.org.

Harmony Education Center. n.d. "Consultancy Protocol." National School Reform Faculty. Accessed March 8, 2024. nsrfharmony.org/wp-content/uploads/2017/10/consultancy_0.pdf.

hooks, bell. 1994. *Teaching to Transgress: Education as the Practice of Freedom*. London: Routledge.

Ladson-Billings, Gloria. 1995. "Toward a Theory of Culturally Relevant Pedagogy." *American Education Research Journal* 32 (3): 465–491. doi.org/10.2307/1163320.

Love, Bettina A. 2019. *We Want to Do More Than Survive: Abolitionist Teaching and the Pursuit of Educational Freedom*. Boston, MA: Beacon Press.

Love, Bettina A. 2023. *Punished for Dreaming: How School Reform Harms Black Children and How We Heal*. New York: St. Martin's Press.

Mapp, Karen. 2003. "Having Their Say: Parents Describe Why and How They Are Engaged in Their Children's Learning." *School Community Journal* 13 (1): 35–64.

Marzano, Robert. 2012. *Becoming a Reflective Teacher*. Bloomington, IN: Marzano Research Laboratory.

Moll, Luis C. 2019. "Elaborating Funds of Knowledge: Community-Oriented Practices in International Contexts." *Literacy Research: Theory, Method, and Practice* 68 (1): 130–138.

Muhammad, Gholdy. 2020. *Cultivating Genius: An Equity Framework for Culturally and Historically Responsive Literacy*. New York: Scholastic.

Muhammad, Gholdy. 2023. *Unearthing Joy: A Guide to Culturally and Historically Responsive Curriculum and Instruction*. New York: Scholastic.

Najarro, Ileana. 2022. "Here's How Many Hours a Week Teachers Work." *Education Week*. April 14, 2022. edweek.org/teaching-learning/heres-how-many-hours-a-week-teachers-work/2022/04.

Noddings, Nel. 1984. *Caring: A Feminine Approach to Ethics and Moral Education*. Oakland, CA: University of California Press.

Rolón-Dow, Rosalie. 2021. "Theorizing Racial Microaffirmations: A Critical Race/LatCrit Approach." *Race, Ethnicity and Education* 24 (2): 245–261. doi.org/10.1080/13613324.2020.1798381.

Rolón-Dow, Rosalie. 2022. "At the Root of Their Stories: Black and LatinX Students' Experiences with Academic Microaggressions." *Harvard Educational Review* 92 (4): 508–532. doi.org/10.17763/1943-5045-92.4.508.

Soslau, Elizabeth. 2015a. "Exploring Intersubjectivity between Student Teachers and Field Instructors in Student Teaching Conferences." *Cogent Education* 2 (1): 1–8. doi.org/10.1080/2331186X.2015.1045219.

Soslau, Elizabeth. 2015b. "Development of a Post-Lesson Observation Conferencing Protocol: Situated in Theory, Research, and Practice." *Teaching and Teacher Education* 49: 22–35. doi.org/10.1016/j.tate.2015.02.012.

Soslau, Elizabeth, Stephanie Kotch-Jester, Kathryn Scantlebury, and Sue Gleason. 2019. "Coteachers' Huddles: Developing Adaptive Teaching Expertise during Student Teaching." *Teaching and Teacher Education* 73: 99–108. doi.org/10.1016/j.tate.2018.03.016.

Soslau, Elizabeth, and Monique Alexander. 2021. *The Comprehensive Guide to Working with Student Teachers: Tools and Templates to Support Reflective Growth*. New York: Teachers College Press.

Stevenson, Howard C. 2014. *Promoting Racial Literacy in Schools: Differences That Make a Difference*. New York: Teachers College Press.

Style, Emily. (1988) 1996. "Curriculum as Window and Mirror." *Social Science Record*.

YouthTruth. 2022. "Insights from the Student Experience, Part I: Emotional and Mental Health." Fall 2022. The Center for Effective Philanthropy, Inc. youthtruthsurvey.org/wp-content/uploads/2023/07/EMH_2022.pdf.

Index

f denotes figure

A

AAVE (African American Vernacular English), 97–98

"About Me and My Family" questionnaire, 79–81

adaptive teaching expertise, 5, 6

"Administrator Report," 129

administrators, relationships with, 40, 58–61

affection, as ingredient in recipe for addressing problematic situations with colleagues, 97, 98, 99

affirming classrooms, 79–81

African American Vernacular English (AAVE), 97–98

Alexander, Monique, 49

"All About Me: Special Skills and Interests" questionnaire, 10–11, 26

anonymous mailbox, 82–84

aspirations, setting yearlong ones for curriculum and learning at new position, 122–124

B

Bandura, Albert, 104, 135

Bernardi, Michelle, 58

Bishop, Rudine Sims, 71

Brave Community: Teaching for a Post-Racist Imagination (Novais), 99

Brown, Brené, 104, 135

burnout, warding off, 105–109

C

calendar, in classroom to indicate visitors, 42

care. *See also* self-care
   having high expectations and holding students accountable for working hard as expression of, 69
   love and care for students (Teacher Spotlight), 70–71
   recognizing importance of demonstrating of for students, 70–71
   for students, examples of, 72–73

challenges, strategies for navigating, 95–110

"Classroom Spaces Inventory," 80*f*, 92

classroom visits, arranging of for family adults, 42

classrooms
   inventorying spaces in, 80
   making all classroom spaces affirming places, 79–81
   setting norms together to build classroom community, 84–86
   strategies for transitioning to new ones, 115–126
   visiting and starting planning for new ones, 124–125

Coalition of Essential Schools, 54

collaboration
   as essential, 39–63
   "Points of Collaboration Reflection Questions," 106*f*, 112

collaborative expertise, 5, 6–7, 95–96

colleagues
   building partnerships with, 48–52
   recipe for addressing problematic situations with, 96–101

common truths, about teaching and learning, 8

communications
   "Family Communication Preferences Chart," 19*f*, 33
   navigating teacher-family communications, 45–47

"Community Asset Planning," 14*f*, 29

community assets/resources
   concentric map of, 13*f*, 28
   discovery of, 12–14
   tapping into, 14

The Comprehensive Guide to Working with Student Teachers (Soslau and Alexander), 49

connection, as ingredient in recipe for addressing problematic situations with colleagues, 97, 98, 100

control, reality check on what's in your control, 109

correction, as ingredient in recipe for addressing problematic situations with colleagues, 97, 98, 99–100
co-teaching, 101–102
counseling, professional, 107
countdown visual, in classroom to indicate visitors, 42
curriculum
    investigation of, at new position, 121–122
    setting yearlong aspirations for, at new position, 122–124

D
dual roles, embodiment of, 7
Dunne, Faith, 54

E
educational materials, as serving as mirrors, windows, and sliding glass doors, 71–72
efficacy, importance of, 7
Epstein, Joyce, 39, 135
Evans, Paula, 54
expectations
    examples of, 23
    family expectations. *See* family expectations
    having high ones as expression of love and care, 69
    matched with goals, 24
expertise
    adaptive teaching expertise, 5, 6
    collaborative expertise, 5, 6–7, 95–96
    emboldening yourself to contribute yours, 103–105
    "Family Expertise Planning Chart," 41f, 64
    types and development of teaching expertise, 5–6

F
family adults
    having students interview them, 15
    inviting them to share their expertise with the class, 40–42
family arrangements, terms used to refer to, 15
"Family Communication Preferences Chart," 19f, 33
family expectations
    analysis of responses to "Family Expectations Questionnaire," 16–19
    examples of, 23

"Family Expectations Questionnaire," 15–16, 30–31
    following up with families regarding, 20
    helping students learn them and set goals, 21–24
    identification of, 15–16
    matched with goals, 24
"Family Expectations Questionnaire," 15–16, 30–31
"Family Expertise Planning Chart," 41f, 64
"Family Follow-Up Letter," 20f–21f
family participation invitation, 41–42
family visits, guiding students to reflect on, 43–44
feedback
    administrator reports as, 119
    peer reports as, 118–119
    tips for responding to feedback from principals, 60–61
first-time observation, Teacher Spotlight on, 61
"Framing a Problem of Practice," 55f–56f
funds of knowledge
    defined, 10
    "Fifth Grade Funds of Knowledge Reflection Chart," 11f
    "Funds of Knowledge Reflection Chart," 12, 27
    unearthing students' funds of knowledge, 10–12
"Funds of Knowledge Reflection Chart," 12, 27

G
gallery walk, for display of people posters, 75
goals
    helping students set goals, 21–24
    matched with expectations, 24
    "My Goal for School," 24, 36
    "Planning and Reaching My Goal," 24, 37
    wish list of student learning goals, 123
goodbyes
    meaningful ones (Teacher Spotlight), 117
    reflecting and planning to make them meaningful, 116–117
Google Docs, 11
Google Translate, 15
Gorman, Amanda, 98–99
Greater Good in Education, 81–82
Greater Good Science Center (University of California–Berkeley), 81
growth competence, as type of teaching expertise, 5–6
growth opportunities, embrace of, 95–109

H

Hall-Russell, Jaela, 58
Harmony Education Center (National School Reform Faculty), 54
help-seeking, as key part of professional practice, 101–103
"The Hill We Climb" (Gorman), 98
hooks, bell, 69, 104–105, 135
huddles, use of, 101–102

I

I Wish I Had... (Teacher Spotlight), 96
identity/identities
    according to Muhammad, 73
    helping students consider how they see themselves and how others see them, 76–79
    helping students express and share theirs, 73–75
    strategies for affirming student identity and belonging, 69–93
    "Student Identity Data Chart," 80f, 91
"Inquiry Group Invitation," 53f–54f

J

Jones, Erik, 58
journaling
    about goals, at new position, 123–124
    how to respond to sensitive or disturbing topics in journals, 83
    in preparation for saying goodbye, 116–117
    "Prompts for Two-Way Journaling," 82f
    to redress missed opportunities to speak up and out, 100–101
    two-way journals, 81–82

L

Ladson-Billings, Gloria, 39–40, 135
learning
    common truths about, 8
    the hard way, 104
    making time for summer learning for yourself, 125–126
learning conditions, for teachers, 7
letter writing, anonymous mailbox, 82–84
letters of recommendation, 120
literature, as serving as mirrors, windows, and sliding glass doors, 71–72
love
    and care for students (Teacher Spotlight), 70–71
    and care in teaching, 69–93
    having high expectations and holding students accountable for working hard as expression of, 69
    recognizing importance of demonstrating of for students, 70–71
Love, Bettina, 69, 136

M

Mapp, Karen, 39, 136
Marzano, Robert, 40, 136
microaffirmations, 99
microaggressions, 99
mirrors, benefits of for students, 71
Moll, Luis, 10, 136
Muhammad, Gholdy, 69, 73, 136
"My Goal for School," 24, 36
"My Plan for Joyful Task Completion," 109, 113
"My Questions for a Treasured Adult," 22, 34–35

N

National School Reform Faculty, Harmony Education Center, 54
new beginnings, preparing for, 120–122
Noddings, Nel, 69, 136
norms
    "Norms Questionnaire," 85, 93
    "Sample Norms Word Cloud," 85f
    "Sample Seventh Grade Classroom Norms," 86f
    setting of to build classroom community, 84–86
"Norms Questionnaire," 85, 93
Novais, Janine de, 99

O

observation
    first-time observation (Teacher Spotlight), 61
    peer observations, 48–52, 65, 118
    selective verbatim as observation note-taking approach, 49
opportunities
    embrace of growth opportunities, 95–109
    journaling to redress missed opportunities to speak up and out, 100–101
    "Redressing Missed Opportunities," 111

P

"Parent-Reported Student Challenges/Areas of Acceleration and Expected Supports," 17f, 32

parents
reaching out to (Teacher Spotlight), 16
as teachers, 44–45
parent-teacher relationships, importance of strong ones, 39
"Peer Observation Form," 65, 118
peer observations
for building partnerships with colleagues, 48–52
"Peer Observation Form," 65, 118
"Peer Report," 119, 127–128
people posters ("This Is Me"), 73–74
"Planning and Reaching My Goal," 24, 37
"Points of Collaboration Reflection Questions," 106f, 112
portfolio
expansion of yours, 118–120
planning of, 120
"Sample Portfolio Tracking Form," 121f, 130
"Portfolio Tracking Form," 121f, 130
preparation, strategies for school year preparation, 9–25
principals
do's and don'ts for building positive relationship with, 62
reflecting on relationship you want with, 63
tips for responding to feedback from, 60–61
problematic situations with colleagues, recipe for addressing, 96–101
professional counseling, 107
"Prompts for Two-Way Journaling," 82f
protection, as ingredient in recipe for addressing problematic situations with colleagues, 97, 98, 100

Q

questionnaires
"About Me and My Family" questionnaire, 79–81
"All About Me: Special Skills and Interests," 10–11
"Family Expectations Questionnaire," 15–16, 30–31
"Norms Questionnaire," 85, 93

R

recommendation, letters of, 120
"Redressing Missed Opportunities," 111
"Reflection on a Problem of Practice: Questions to Consider," 55, 66

relationships
with administrators, 40, 58–61, 62, 63
early relationship building at new position, 121
parent-teacher relationships, 39
resources, discovering community assets, 12–14
rituals of practice, as component of self-care, 108–109
Rolón-Dow, Rosalie, 99

S

"Sample Administrator Report Details," 119f
"Sample Norms Word Cloud," 85f
"Sample Portfolio Tracking Form," 121f
"Sample Seventh Grade Classroom Norms," 86f
school year preparation, strategies for, 9–25
selective verbatim, as observation note-taking approach, 49
self-actualization
reflection questions about, 106f
striving toward, 104–105
self-care
importance of, 106–107
infusing joy through small acts of, 108
rituals of practice as component of, 108–109
Teacher Spotlight on, 108
self-efficacy
growing a sense of, 105
reflection questions about, 106f
sensitive or disturbing topics (in journals), how to respond to, 83
shout-out box, for student affirmations, 86–87
sliding doors, benefits of for students, 71–72
SMART method, 24
starting out, Teacher Spotlight, 1
Stevenson, Howard, 96–97, 136
stress, management of, 105–109
student affirmations, having shout-out box for, 86–87
"Student Feelings Tally," 17f
student identity and belonging, strategies for affirming, 69–93
"Student Identity Data Chart," 80f, 91
Style, Emily, 71
"Summary of a Basic Protocol for a Teacher Inquiry Group," 54f–55f
support
beyond school, 107–108
at school, 107

When You're the New Teacher

T

teacher inquiry group
  defined, 52
  following meeting protocol of, 57–58
  forming of, 52–53
  invitation to, 53f–54f
  preparing for meeting of, 55
  setting meeting protocol for, 54
  "Summary of a Basic Protocol for a
    Teacher Inquiry Group," 54f–55f
teacher-family communications, navigation
  of, 45–47
teacher(s)
  parents as, 44–45
  positioning yourself as, 7
teaching
  common truths about, 8
  expanding your portfolio in, 118–120
  finding joy in, 105–109
  love and care in, 69–93
teaching expertise, types and development of,
  5–6
"This Is Me" people posters, 73–74, 75f, 78,
  88
Thompson-Grove, Gene, 54
transitioning
  to new classroom, school, or role,
    115–126

Teacher Spotlight on, 116
treasured adults
  defined, 21
  having students share their goal-settings
    plans with, 24, 37
  "My Questions for a Treasured Adult,"
    22, 34–35
  preparing students to interview them,
    21–22

U

University of California–Berkeley, Greater
  Good Science Center, 81

V

vulnerability
  reflection questions about, 106f
  sharing ideas and, 104

W

"What's the Dilemma? Summary and Details
  about a Problem of Practice," 55, 67
"Who Is the Me That Others See?," 78, 89–90
windows, benefits of for students, 71

Digital Resources

Accessing the Digital Resources

The digital resources can be downloaded by following these steps:

1. Go to **www.tcmpub.com/digital**
2. Use the 13-digit ISBN number to redeem the digital resources.
3. Respond to the question using the book.
4. Follow the prompts on the Content Cloud website to sign in or create a new account.
5. The content redeemed will appear on your My Content screen. Click on the product to look through the digital resources. All file resources are available for download. Select files can be previewed, opened, and shared. Any web-based content, such as videos, links, or interactive text, can be viewed and used in the browser but is not available for download.

For questions and assistance with your ISBN redemption, please contact Teacher Created Materials.

email: customerservice@tcmpub.com
phone: 800-858-7339

About the Author

Dr. Elizabeth Soslau is a professor in the School of Education at the University of Delaware. She focuses her teaching, research, and service efforts on *tzedakah* (justice) and *tikkun olam* (repair the world). Her research focuses on experiential learning opportunities in classrooms, schools, and the community. Elizabeth seeks to explore and enhance teaching practices that support teachers' and students' understandings of systemic social ills, develop critical consciousness, and strengthen their voice and activism skills.

She is the coauthor of *The Comprehensive Guide to Working with Student Teachers* (Teachers College Press). Her work has appeared in outlets such as the *Journal of Teacher Education, Teaching and Teacher Education, Journal for Multicultural Education, Journal of Community Engagement and Scholarship,* and *The Jewish Exponent*. She is also a reviewer for numerous journals, a long-time board member of the Philadelphia-based nonprofit Need in Deed, and serves on the International Advisory Board for the *Studying Teacher Education* journal. Her clinical work includes teaching graduate and undergraduate courses in critical reflection, equity, urban education, case study methods, and action research.

Elizabeth's other important work is serving as a very proud mother of the hilarious and creative Harry Counter. She is also a dedicated partner to Chris Counter. Before pursuing her Ph.D., Elizabeth taught middle school in the School District of Philadelphia. She lives and works in the Delaware Valley area.